Real Life Stories

Inmate to Inmate

Let the redeemed of the LORD tell their story—
those he redeemed from the hand of the foe,

Psalm10

Real People
in
Real Places
with
Real Problems
Looking for a
Real Answer

*People so Real that it could
be someone that you know.*

Table of Contents

Additional Table of Contents

CHAPTER 1
I Was Mad
At The World...

...at myself, and at God

I became so helpless and hopeless that I was lost in despair.

My name is Jeremy. I was born in 1979 in Indianapolis, Indiana. From the time I was born to age 6, I witnessed my father abuse my mother. It was bad enough at times that they both would have to go to the hospital. One evening during that time, my father was drunk...again. He hit my mother....again. Finally, she had enough. After he passed out on the couch in the living room, she took charcoal lighter fluid and set my father on fire.

You may be going through something similar. There are people who have been there, and we are called to help our fellow man.

After their divorce, my father drifted in and out of my life. He spent most of his time drunk or in jail for drinking. My mother went on a downward spiral, and she began using drugs. This was a terrible time for me and my sister, who was two years older. My mother's goal in life was to forget her pain by getting high. She did whatever it took to get high. She even prostituted herself for drugs. My sister and I spent the next few years in an environment where we were filthy, hardly fed, and abused. There was a male "babysitter" who used to hit me, lock me in the cabinet under the kitchen sink, and put me in an ice cold bath. He would choke me until I almost passed out and then let me go. He laughed hysterically as I gasped for air. Luckily, my sister was mostly unharmed during this time.

We witnessed constant drug abuse as well as sexual situations that children at 8 and 10 years old shouldn't see. Finally, a neighbor called the police about the situation my sister and I were in. They came and removed us from the house when my mother wasn't home. No one knew where she was. She had been arrested for prostitution.

We were placed in a foster home where we were loved and cared for. This was the best time of our lives. After about eight months, the court determined that we should be returned to our mother after she was released from jail. She had cleaned the house and bought a hot plate to cook on.

During her incarceration, my mother met a man whom she had known in her youth. He had family in California, and they decided it would be best for us all to move out there for a fresh start. This new man was a stable influence on my mother. She gave up all the harder drugs but continued to drink and smoke marijuana. After almost two years in California, we all moved back to Indiana. My mother got married to this man. He was a good provider who met our physical needs. During this time, we were only abused emotionally and mentally. We were constantly called worthless and "no good" by our mother and stepfather.

We lived a few blocks from my grandparents. My Mom's Dad was a Christian man. He convinced me to go to church with him. I began spending more time with him and learning about God. We enjoyed our time together. My grandparents ended up moving, and we stopped going to church together and drifted apart.

About this time, I began trying different drugs. I was getting high every day. I didn't care about anything anymore. I was angry and frustrated. It seemed to me that anytime I was in a good place, like foster care or with my grandfather, something happened to take it all away. I began to blame God.

While I was being fueled by drugs and the need to get more, I began stealing and robbing people. I wanted money and to experience the emotional high I wasn't getting at home. I didn't want to be there anymore. I became all about myself in everything I did. No one mattered but me.

When I was 14 years old, I went to live with my father. He had remarried and given up drinking. He was a totally different person now that he wasn't drinking. We got along well, and my stepmother was a blessing. She was encouraging. I hadn't experienced this before.

I continued to get high and get into trouble. I got arrested twice for stealing cars and finally got arrested for armed robbery when I was 15 years old. I went to a juvenile correctional facility for two years. While I was inside, I attended school. When I was released at 17, I returned to school and graduated from high school.

I was now living back with my mother and stepfather. I was working two jobs and trying to make a way for myself, but I couldn't agree with my parents. My stepfather and I argued so much that at one point he told my mother that either I had to leave or he would leave. So, when I was still 17 years old, my mother kicked me out. I bounced from place to place and stayed with an uncle or a friend. I continued to use drugs, steal, and rob.

A few weeks before I turned 19, I robbed the convenience store where I worked and murdered a co-worker. I am now 32 years old. I am serving life without parole, and I have been incarcerated since 1998. Since I have been here, I have earned two college degrees. I have an Associate's in Arts and a Bachelor's in General Studies with concentrations in History and Computers. I have held different jobs here at the prison since I graduated. I recently took a job in the prison furniture factory. It is one of the best places to be in this prison. I am currently working on an apprenticeship for Office Management in collusion with my job. It is a wonderful program sponsored by the U.S. Department of Labor.

In April of 2005, I accepted Jesus Christ as my personal Savior. My first 6-7 years in prison were punctuated by drugs, gangs, and violence. I was mad at myself, at the world, and at God. In 2005, I became so helpless and hopeless that I was in despair. I began reading the old tattered Bible my mom sent me when I got arrested in 1998. I knew a lot of the Word but had neglected it. After weeks of reading it, I was so convicted within myself. I knelt before the Lord in my cell and begged Him for forgiveness. My burden was lifted. I felt amazingly free and light-hearted.

Since that time I have continued to pursue my life in Christ. I study

Scripture every day and open my heart to the Lord in prayer. I spend time fellowshipping with my Christian Brothers here at the prison. I spend a great deal of time at the Religious Services Center. I attend a non-denominational service. I serve as a lay leader for this service, which simply means I direct the service. I am one of five chosen to do so out of 100 congregation members. We keep the service on track and make sure it runs smoothly, introducing each individual as his time comes up. I feel really blessed to be able to serve my Christian community in here. I also attend a Bible study as well. One of my favorite things is the Kairos service I attend weekly. It is a prayer & share meeting for all of the Kairos graduates to get together and fellowship. Kairos is a prison ministry that holds weekend events at different prisons. Offenders are selected to attend for the entire weekend. Volunteers come in and feed you, minister to you, and generally just show the love of Jesus Christ.

My time began with hatred toward others, toward myself, and toward God. I was filled with hopelessness and despair. It became too much to bear. Christ accepted me and forgave me. I am free of my burden. Jesus saved me. He has the power to save every one of us, including those in prison. My purpose now is to tell everyone how God has taken away my pain, bitterness, and stress. It is my purpose to tell every man and woman in prison that Jesus Christ died for all of our sins. I gave Him a chance. Please do the same. God bless you all.

— *Jeremy*

CHAPTER 2
My Encounter With
The Presence Of God

As a young child, I remember my mother reading to me from a picture bible about God. Around the age of eight, I remember repeating some words in church and weeping as I asked Jesus into my heart and into my life.

When I was around the age of twelve, I went with a church for the weekend to a "Pow-Wow." It was starting to get dark as we walked up the path to a large bonfire. Coming upon the scene, we saw people young and old walking up to a rope that enclosed this bonfire. On the other side of the rope, men were standing there boldly speaking in tongues. With an outstretched arm, they would put their hand in front of each individual's forehead that approached the rope. Within seconds, the people would fall straight back and hit the ground without anyone touching them and without anyone catching them before hitting the ground.

I truly didn't understand what I was witnessing, but I wanted to try it because something about it seemed so profound. I left my brothers standing there along with Joe, the man who took us, walked up to the rope, and waited anxiously for the man to come before me. I didn't know what I would truly experience.

As the anticipation grew, I started to have a feeling of fear come over me. I was about to run back over to my brothers. Before I could, there he was in front of me, with his hand only a few inches from my forehead. He was boldly speaking in this unknown language. All of a sudden, my fear dissipated. I was in pure bliss as I was being laid down by three people on both sides of me.

I could not make out the faces because the light from the bonfire was so bright. Once I finally reached the ground, I looked around to see the people who had laid me down and nobody was around me. I got up and ran back to my brothers and Joe, asking who it was that caught me. They said nobody touched me. They said they watched me fall back and hit the ground like everyone else. I didn't believe them until Joe explained it to me. It wasn't people that caught me. It was God's angels. This encounter with the presence of God has been the anchor of my soul, knowing that such a real and divine God does exist.

Throughout many of my teenage and young adult years I willingly indulged a life with drugs. This led to near death encounters on several occasions. These "wake-up" moments, however, were not enough to deter me from living a life running in the opposite direction of God. There were so many other times throughout my life that I was spared, and I know it was only by the Grace of God.

At the age of 29, I read Mark 16:16 in the KJV Bible, "Whoever believes and is baptized will be saved, but whoever does not believe will be condemned. "I continued my research about baptism. In Acts 2:38 after the sinners asked "What shall we do?" Peter replied, "Repent, and be baptized every one of you in the name of Jesus Christ for the remission of sins, and ye shall receive the gift of the Holy Ghost." This one verse has changed my whole life. That very moment I knew that I wanted to be baptized in the name of Jesus Christ. Right then, I told God that I repent of all my sins and that I would do my best to follow Him. I told Him that I wanted to receive the gift of the Holy Ghost. Soon after that, I was baptized in His name. I really didn't feel any different afterwards, but I knew that I had followed His command.

A few months later, around 2:00 A.M., I awoke from a deep sleep with tears streaming down both sides of my face. I was speaking in another language, one that I had never heard of nor spoke in before. I knew that this was the promise God made to me in His Word, the gift of the Holy Ghost (Acts 2:38). The gift of tongues (tongues: 1 Cor. 14:18 & 1 Cor. 12:10) has been permanently imparted to me

from Him, and it is my personal prayer language between Go
I. Every morning and throughout the entire day, the Holy Spirit gi
me utterance to speak in tongues. I do this in faith, knowing that .
is Spirit to Spirit communion and worship with my Lord and Savior.
Since then, my desire to know God has increased dramatically. I have
sought Him diligently through fasting, praying, and the study of His
Word. I love to know that I am always in His presence, no matter
where I am or what I am going through. There really is a peace that
only He can give you.

I would like to share with you 15 verses from the KJV Bible that has
transformed many lives, and yours could be one of them:

1. For all have sinned, and come short of the glory of God; (Romans
   3:23)
2. For the wages of sin is death; but the gift of God is eternal life
   through Jesus Christ our Lord. (Romans 6:26) 6:23
3. ...Believe on the Lord Jesus Christ, and thou shalt be saved, and
   thy house. (Acts 16:31)
4. ...Repent, and be baptized every one of you in the name of Jesus
   Christ for the remission of sins, and ye shall receive the gift of the
   Holy Ghost. (Acts 2:38)
5. For by grace are ye saved through faith; and that not of yourselves:
   it is the gift of God: Not of works, lest any man should boast.
   (Ephesians 2:8-9)
6. That if thou shalt confess with thy mouth the Lord Jesus, and shalt
   believe in thine heart that God hath raised him from the dead, thou
   shalt be saved. For with the heart man believeth unto righteousness;
   and with the mouth confession is made unto salvation. For
   whosoever shall call upon the name of the Lord shall be saved.
   (Romans 10:9,10,13)
7. And the publican, standing afar off, would not lift up so much as
   his eyes unto heaven, but smote upon his breast, saying, God be
   merciful to me a sinner. (Luke 18:13)
8. For God so loved the world, that he gave his only begotten Son, that
   whosoever believeth in him should not perish, but have everlasting
   life. For God sent not his Son into the world to condemn the world;

world through him might be saved. (John 3:16-17)

...suaded, that neither death, nor life, nor angels, nor ...nor powers, nor things present, nor things to come, ...depth, nor any other creature, shall be able to ...the love of God, which is in Christ Jesus our Lord. ...ans 8:38-39)

10. My sheep hear my voice and I know them, and they follow me; And I give unto them eternal life; and they shall never perish, neither shall any man pluck them out of my hand. My Father, which gave them me, is greater than all; and no man is able to pluck them out of my Father's hand. I and my Father are one. (John 10:27-30)

11. For he saith, I have heard thee in a time accepted, and in the day of salvation have I succored thee: behold, now is the accepted time; behold, now is the day of salvation. (2 Corinthians 6:2)

12. He that believeth and is baptized shall be saved; but he that believeth not shall be damned. (Mark 16:16)

13. But these are written, that ye might believe that Jesus is the Christ, the Son of God; and that believing ye might have life through his name. (John 20:31)

14. Let your light so shine before men, that they may see your good works, and glorify your Father which is in heaven. (Matthew 5:16)

15. For whosoever will save his life shall lose it: but whosoever will lose his life for my sake, the same shall save it. For what is a man advantaged, if he gain the whole world, and lose himself, or be cast away? For whosoever shall be ashamed of me and of my words, of him shall the Son of man be ashamed, when he shall come in his own glory, and in his Father's, and of the holy angels. (Luke 9:24-26)

Time is short. I ask you to share these verses with your loved ones and with anyone that God lays on your heart. God says that His Word does not return to him void. His Word will complete its purpose.

— *Eric*

CHAPTER 3
I Gambled And
Lost So Much...

I was becoming an addict.

I would drink and use drugs to calm my nerves...

After a nine-year marriage and one beautiful child (Leah), my obsession with darts had finally caught up to me. The game of darts was my obsession. I loved the game so much. I have received multiple state titles, a couple of national titles, and a couple of world titles playing electronic darts. In the year 2000, I had taken 1st place in the world in a non-pro singles, 501 dart event with over 500 entries. The tournament was held in Chicago, Illinois. A few years before that in a national tournament, I had taken 1st place in a four-man event in Las Vegas. During my life of darts, I did not realize it, but I was becoming an addict. I would drink and use drugs to calm my nerves. It seemed to be the answer to all my problems, or was it?

During my dart playing years, I lost my marriage of nine years. I lost many jobs because I was often too hung-over to make it to work after a weekend of drinking and drugging. I ended up getting a divorce and moved in with a girl I had met. From there, things seemed to get worse. I eventually left that relationship after about two years. From there I ended up moving out of state to Indiana with a friend's parents. I felt that if I got away from everything, I could get my life back on track. My philosophy worked for a bit, but soon I was back to my own self, darting, drinking, and drugging.

To fast forward ahead a bit, I had gotten remarried and inherited three more wonderful children. Both my and my wife's habit, became too expensive, so a person whom we thought was a friend suggested we start selling drugs for him. In return, we would never have to pay for our habit. "It would also provide additional income for us," he said. That night we talked about it, and soon after we took on the offer. Shortly thereafter, my wife and I were both arrested for dealing and possession charges. We were sent to jail.

While in the county jail, wondering who would take care of our children and how soon it would be before we were released, we found out that our charges were very serious. I am talking up to 50 year sentence. Devastated by the news, family stepped in and solved the children problem. Our children were now in good hands. Our next problem was that the house we were renting was full with all our stuff. What were we going to do? We didn't have the money to pay the rent. We were not expected to go to trial for a few months. Meanwhile, our landlord was not receiving any rent for the time we were locked up.

As I was sitting there in the county jail one afternoon, about three weeks after being arrested, my landlord came to see me. He asked me what my plans were as far as moving our stuff out. I had told him that we did not have any family close enough to move us out of his place, and I did not know what we were going to do. My fear at that moment was that our landlord was going to tell me that if we didn't get all of our stuff out of there by the time our rent was due, he would throw all our stuff out by the curb. Instead, my landlord asked me when our court date was. I told him that it was scheduled in a few months. He told me he would go home and talk to his wife to see what kind of arrangements could be worked out. Thinking the worst, I was sick to my stomach. I didn't know where to turn. It was later that night that I got down on my knees and prayed. I was never much of a religious person, but I didn't know where else to turn. I said to God, "Look, I don't know if you are real, but if you are, and you can hear me, I need your help!" The following day my landlord came to see me. He told me his wife was also there to visit with my wife. Again, I though the worst. During our conversation, my landlord kept telling me not to worry about our stuff. He said that he and his wife had talked and they would wait to see what happened at our court date. I reminded him that our court date was months away. He said that our stuff would be fine, all of it would be moved to the basement, and that he would lock it up down there until we found out our fate. I told him that we were sorry but we did not have any rent money for him. He said he would worry about that later and then asked me how I was doing. he asked me if I needed anything. I could not believe my ears. I owed this man rent money and he was asking me if I am okay, and do I need anything. The first thing that came to mind was the prayer I prayed the night before. It was at that moment that a feeling came over me. "Is all this stuff about God real?" I asked myself. "Did He hear my prayers last night?" I didn't know what was going on, but things were all working out for us. The kids were all in good hands, and the problem with our landlord was working out. As my landlord was leaving from the visit, he said that he had left something at the front desk for me. He said that my wife would also receive something. I told him goodbye and thanked him. As I returned to my jail cell, an officer came to the dorm and gave me a Bible. He said that it was from the person who had just came to visit me. Again, I could not believe what was going on. Why is this person who barely knows me, and whom I owe money to, being so nice to me? I spent the night reading that Bible, and it was shortly after that time that I gave my life to Christ. I wanted to have the kind of love that my landlord had for us.

When you give your life to Jesus Christ, you inherit His Light. You display that Light when you exhibit love. When you exhibit love, you lead others to Christ.

— *R.B.*

The Truth

The people you have just read about had to come to a place of knowing, understanding, and accepting the truth before their lives could be changed.

Throughout the rest of this book, in between the many more "Real Life Stories," we will share some of these truths with you.

God's Law

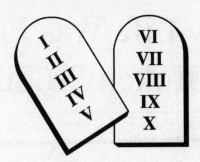

THE TEN COMMANDMENTS

1 You shall have no other gods before me

2 You shall not make yourself any graven image

3 You shall not take the Name of the Lord your God in vain

4 Remember the Sabbath Day to keep it holy

5 Honor your father and mother

6 You shall not kill

7 You shall not commit adultery

8 You shall not steal

9 You shall not lie

10 You shall not covet

Each of the people you have read about had to face God's Law.

Have You Obeyed God's Law?

Are You Sure?

You can go to the next page and read several more "Real Life Stories" or you can skip ahead to our next truth on page 36.

CHAPTER 4
My Life Was Full
Of Broken Promises

Something happened to me...

I became full of hate, bitterness, and resentment.

I'm a fifty-one year old retired Rodeo cowboy. My childhood was as normal as it could be for a kid with no father and a mother who battled alcoholism and depression. I was raised by my grandparents. We lived on a small farm in Central Indiana and lived off the land with hunting, fishing, and lots of hard work. My grandmother was the sweetest lady that I have ever met, and she never met a stranger. My grandfather was a good man who believed in working hard and handing out many chores to do. However, when he drank, he had a mean streak. We got along fine while I was a child, working, hunting, and fishing together. He would listen to my stories of someday being a Rodeo Cowboy.

My childhood ended when I was nine years old with a phone call from my mom. She was drunk and depressed. She wanted to talk to me, but my grandmother wouldn't wake me because it was late. I woke up to the commotion on the phone. Just as I picked up the other line, I heard the gunshot. My mother took her life, and that was the end of my childhood. I know my family meant well, but for the next few years my life was full of broken promises. One after another promised to take me into their family, when all I wanted was for things to be like they used to be.

I became full of hate, bitterness, and resentment. My relationship with my grandparents was never the same. I became very dark, isolating myself for hours and sometimes days in my room. I was so rebellious that my grandfather had no choice but to discipline me the only way he knew how; in the form of beating with a fist, switch, or a whip. I will admit that most of them, I deserved.

I was fourteen when I left home the first time, chasing the dream of being a cowboy. I ended up working for a Wild West show and Rodeo, living like a "Carney" on the fair circuit. I was way too young and small to be on my own. While hitchhiking that year, I was raped by a truck-driver. This fed my lack of trust and my anger, but I never let it stop me. I would come home in the fall and fulfill the promise made to my grandmother to finish school, leaving again in the spring.

I loved being on the road and riding bareback, horses, and bulls. The road became my escape. I had no idea how to find what I was looking for at that time in my life, so what I found was meth. I was fifteen years old, angry, bitter, and feeling rejected. The only thing that I found to kill my pain was drugs. I continued on this path of destruction for the next few years, and then after some surgeries became addicted to Demerol and Morphine. I spiraled out of control for the next few years, chasing my dream of being a champion. I would do speed to wake me up so I could ride, then take pain killers to kill the pain. And of course, like my mother and grandfather, alcohol became a factor also.

I ended up being just like them. I was a mean drunk, full of hate, and I had no problem showing it. The void in my life was never going to be filled with drugs or alcohol. I knew nothing of God or Jesus, other than cowboys praying before they would ride. These same cowboys would be in the bar chasing tail after the rodeo. In my eyes, they were a joke. I persecuted and made fun of them and their God.

I believe it was 1981, and I was twenty-one years old. I had been competing on the circuit riding bucking horses and bulls that year. I was riding with a lot of injuries that season, so I decided to enter a rodeo at Davey, Florida. Win, lose, or draw, I was going to take some time off to heal up.

I remember her well. After being thrown off, stomped, and dragged around, I found her standing in the crowd staring at me with her big blue eyes and blond hair. Her name was Jennifer, but I called her Jen.

She was a dancer and loved cocaine. To be honest, I would snort, smoke, or ingest anything that would kill my pain and make me forget the past. She had unlimited access to this drug and turned me on to free-basing.

About one year later and fifty pounds lighter, I was forced to leave my source to this drug that I loved so much. I couldn't work and had no money to support my drug habits. After trying my hand at a few robberies and other stupid things, there I lay under a pier in DT's (withdrawls) with the homeless. This was the last thing I remember until being kicked in the side and awakened.

As I began to move, I realized that I couldn't open my eyes. I felt something moving in my nose and mouth. Flies had begun to work on me, and I had maggots in my mouth and nose. The man who kicked me was a long haired fellow, and he explained to me that he checked for bodies under the piers and tried to help the homeless. He cleaned me up and bought me breakfast. His advice to me was to go back up north where people cared about me. This made sense to me, so off I went hitchhiking to Indiana.

I was jonesing for some cocaine, in DT's and withdrawal from the morphine. I found myself under another bridge on the interstate close to Lakeland, Florida. The only thing left of my past was my rodeo gear bag, a cowboy hat, and of course the pain. I remember being afraid to fall asleep because I might die. Then I heard brakes squealing. A young kid with a cowboy hat backed up to me. He asked if I was a cowboy and needed help. I answered, "Not much of a cowboy, I need a fix."

He took me to his step-dad's church. His name was Mikey, and his step-dad's name was Paul. Paul asked me a very important question that day. He asked if I believed that God could heal me and make me whole again. As I studied the question, it came to me that if God could create the heavens and the earth, He could surely fix me. I spoke those words and was instantly healed. He led me through the sinner's prayer, and I accepted Jesus into my heart that day. Hallelujah! Ain't it funny how God's blessings are there for the taking? Without someone being obedient to God's word and showing compassion to others, I might have died under a bridge that year. Instead, He met me just as I was and sent me three angels.

Over the next year, my faith grew. I began to learn that God loved me and that there was wonder working power in the blood of Jesus. While I lived in Lakeland and was surrounded by a group of believers, I was just fine. However, when I returned to Indiana I fell under condemnation and persecution. Even though I fully intended to do the will of God, Satan had too much fuel. The pain returned in my life, and I began self-medicating again. This time it was marijuana, speed, and pain pills. I stayed high and began drinking again. My life seemed to be like a movie that never ended, no beginning and no end.

I had spurts of happiness over the next several years, moving from church to church and even from state to state trying to forget my childhood and find peace. I still competed on the Rodeo circuit and worked on ranches and farms throughout the years, but something was missing. I began to believe that I needed to get married and settle down. I had two failed marriages and wasn't much of a dad either. I wanted to do the right thing but couldn't seem to love them properly. I had a mean streak, just like my grandfather, and couldn't show anyone love or trust in their love for me. God never left me and through all this, He healed me of a broken back. It was a miracle in my life that I will never forget. I will always give Him praise. He's an awesome God.

I returned to my old lifestyle once again, and this time it was worse than ever. I not only began to use meth again, but this time I began to manufacture the drug. In 2003, after violating probation and being on the run, I was involved in a chase which ended with me running into a house to hide. When forced with the situation of going to prison, I drew a gun and decided to let the police shoot me. They fired fourteen shots at me. I was only hit by a ricocheting bullet, which did not harm me. I was found guilty of twelve felonies. This included two attempted murders, even though I never shot at anyone. I was suicidal, not homicidal. I was sentenced to one-hundred three years in prison.

I became very bitter and mad at God and myself. It seemed to me that I had failed at everything, even my suicide. I wanted nothing to do with God at the time. I turned my back on Him but never forgot what I had experienced and the love I felt in Christ Jesus. The next two years were terrible. I was diagnosed with Prostate Cancer but never had a biopsy. I believed the report and accepted this curse. I lost about fifty pounds and was weakening.

I received a visit from my aunt and daughters one day and was reminded by them of all that God had done for me. Out of the mouth of babes came wisdom and strength. When I returned to my cell, I cried out to God, repented for my disobedience, and rededicated my life to Christ. From that day, I found the will to live and began to thank God for my healing. I spoke healing and broke the curse of cancer in my life. Victory was mine, and I took it.

Over the next few years, I began to submit to God and resisted the devil. He began a great work in me in all areas of my life. I went to a Christian retreat in 2008 and did something that changed my life. I forgave my mom, my grandfather, and everyone who had hurt me. I asked God to forgive me for my unforgivingness, and He healed my heart. A load was lifted off me, and I began to feel love for everyone. I started a greeting ministry at my church to share God's love with everyone else. This year, God blessed me with the opportunity to be in leadership and to share His Word, Love, and testimonies with the men in this prison. God uses the most unlikely of men. He took a broken, hurt, and angry man, and is now using him for His glory. He can use you too. Hallelujah!

— *Cowboy*

CHAPTER 5
Whatever It Takes

As I ponder the years leading up to the present day, a short assignment given to my ninth grade English class makes its way to the front of my mind's eye. It was nothing significant, really. In fact, I don't recall the teacher even grading the paper. But I do remember each student being handed a questionnaire entitled, "Where will you be in ten years?" We were then instructed to answer this question, along with several other related questions, concerning student expectations and prospects of potential status at the conclusion of the decade. Though I cannot say for sure exactly what I wrote, one thing is certain: Never in a thousand lifetimes would I have anticipated I'd be serving a 53 year prison sentence for murder in a state prison.

Obviously, a lot has happened since that carefree day in advanced freshman English class. I can hardly believe that more than ten years have come and gone. It is a truism that our earthly lives are but a vapor that "appeareth for a little time, and then vanisheth away" (Jas.4:14). Had I known then what I know now, I could have spared myself a great many days of evil. Only by the grace of God am I alive to tell my story.

I was raised in church from a very young age. Like most other kids, I went because I had to. I never felt any special connection to God as a child, nor did I in my teenage years. The allures of this world – the lust of the flesh, the lust of the eyes, and the pride of life ruled my young soul. I became sexually active, stopped going to church, and by age 16 was smoking a half pack of Newports a day. A pernicious marijuana habit progressively developed, followed by a raging sex addiction that involved both girlfriends and a steady diet of internet pornography. After high school, I got a job at a large musical instrument retailer and decided to pursue my dream of achieving rock stardom in the entertainment industry. I reasoned that I was smart enough to go to college later if the band didn't work out. In my own mind, I had all the time in the world.

My outgoing personality, strong work ethic, and musical talent helped me become a top sales associate. This in turn afforded me the disposable income needed to live the fast life of sex, drugs, and rock-n-roll that I so eagerly embraced. I supplemented my marijuana use with alcohol, oxycodone, and vicodin. I occasionally experimented with cocaine. Before I knew it, I was going to a clinic each week to be treated with prescription drugs for opiate dependency. By the world's standard, I had everything a 20 year old could want: nice clothes, a new truck, a good job, a successful local band, various female sex partners, etc. However, I was hopelessly miserable. It may have looked good on the outside, like I had it together. Inside, I was dying.

In August of 2006, my poor lifestyle choices launched me into a deep depression that would forever change the course of my life. On top of the opiate "blocker" suboxone (which actually got me just as high as the street drugs), the alcohol, and the marijuana, I had been abusing anabolic steroids for several months. When I stopped taking the shots, the crash was so bad I could hardly get out of bed. I actually wanted to die. One day at work, I became so irritated I decided to walk out on my boss, along with my band mate, friend, and fellow employee. All of this after he got angry over a minor fray with the store manager. Within a few weeks, I got a job working the door at a strip club. A couple of months later, I left there to do part-time construction. Shortly after, that door closed when the boss withdrew from the job site to pursue other endeavors.

It was somewhere around late October/early November when I met Ashley. She was a beautiful blonde 18 year old working as a stripper at a local club. We connected instantly, and within one week were having sex every day. I fell for her so hard it was almost supernatural, as though my will were taken captive under the power of a spell. I wanted to marry her, stop doing drugs, and enjoy a normal life. However, I was no match for the forces working against me. We used drugs together every day and planned to get married in the near future. As the weeks passed, I became more and more disturbed by her occupation. She had already agreed to get another job, but we had just moved into an apartment together. I had many bills backed up from my interim between jobs. I felt utterly emasculated being dependent on a woman for income. The feelings of inadequacy dealt a serious blow to my manhood. This drove me further into drugs and alcohol. I landed a job at a mortgage company as a loan officer. I didn't like it, quit, and got another job as a car salesman. Through the influence of a co-worker, an unseen force spawned in me a waxing interest in witchcraft and the occult. I began to "see" things in the spiritual realm and was on the verge of becoming a practicing warlock when the prayer finally came.

Drowning in a festering cesspool of depression, drugs, and sexual immorality-all alone, I knelt before the crucifix on my wall. Solemnly, with my head bowed, I said to God, "God, please do whatever it takes to fix my life." That was it. That was all I knew to say. Three days later, I found myself in a solitary confinement cell charged with first degree murder.

Of course, I am in no way suggesting God caused me to respond the way I did. I have come to understand that sometimes God must allow us to act outside of His will of desire to honor His law of free will. Terrible atrocities not actively caused by God are often used by Him for a greater good. I do have contrition in my heart, and if there were any way to undo what was done, Lord knows I would. Never would I have planned or purposed to do such evil to another human being- two gunshot wounds to the head, multiple stab wounds to the neck and chest, throat lacerations, the victim's corpse dumped in an alley. The whole ordeal was horrifying beyond belief. I felt like I was living a person's worst nightmare.

The evening before the incident, Ashley and I had been doing ecstasy and cocaine (along with a host of other substances) at our apartment. Later, we were joined by the dealer from whom we had obtained the drugs. He spent the night on the couch. When I awoke the next day, I was confronted by Ashley in the hallway. She started to cry, as we went back into the bedroom. She told me the dealer had raped her while I slept. Things get a little hazy at this point. Though I could say much more, it is not the time to recount the lurid details.

One week after my arrest, I lost the will to live. I took a piece of broken glass from a light fixture in my cell and punctured my left ante-cubical vein. I lost over four pints of blood before I began lapsing out of consciousness. My whole body began to tingle, and it became very hard to breathe. Within minutes, I would be dead. But as fate would have it, it wasn't my time to go. Somehow jail staff discovered me in time. I was rushed by ambulance to a nearby hospital, where I received a blood transfusion and spent the night in intensive care. Soon after returning to the jail, I was ready to pray. I knelt in my cell in front of the iron-barred window and poured out my heart to God. I told Him how sorry I was, and I meant it. I told him He could have me and that I would do whatever He wanted if He would only help me with my situation. Then it happened. A numinous power surged through my body, as the glorious presence of the Holy Spirit enveloped me in a wave of heavenly love. It was as though the Lord Himself were standing invisibly before me. I could not see Him, but I could feel Him. I felt loved unconditionally as a supernatural peace that transcends understanding rested on me. For the first time, I beheld with my spirit the face of infinite love, and I would never be the same again.

A copy of the New Testament made its way to my cell. As I read the four Gospels, the Living Christ stepped out of the pages and into my heart. He has been enthroned and reigning supreme in my life for over 5 years. I was appalled at the filthiness of my sin. Suddenly, I became acutely aware of the need for forgiveness and uncompromisingly resolute in my knowledge of the necessity of Jesus's atoning death as the only means of procuring that forgiveness. This was so profound to me because I was previously convinced that the New Age school of thought – that there are many roads to God and that no single belief system is better than any other – was the right one. However, my encounter with the "One True God" left an indelible mark on my soul that would forever change my secular worldview. I believe with all my heart that Jesus was and is, in fact, the way, the truth, and the life. He is the first and the last, the Alpha and the Omega, the beginning and the end. No one comes to the Father except through Him.

I know this not only because the Bible says so, but because I know Him personally. The veil has been lifted, and my faith has now become empirical knowledge. I have no need to place trust in a mere possibility, relying on anecdotal evidence and wistful sentiments of hope that "there might be a God out there somewhere." The Lord Christ is real. He is not merely a psychological crutch summoned from the figments of an overactive imagination. He is the eternal son of the Most High, the Faithful and True Witness, and the Omnipotent Sovereign of the universe. He is to be feared exceedingly.

Sadly, many today have forgotten the power of the cross. The reality is that without the cross, there is no forgiveness, no life, and no hope. There is only death. Every day I depend on His might for the will to persevere in such a dark place. He is my rock and my salvation, my only source of hope. Without Him, I can do nothing. With Him, I can do all things.

Prison life is not easy. Yet, resting in the shadow of the almighty, I have watched divine providence guard me time and time again. In my 5 years of incarceration, I've been through a riot, endured numerous lockdowns, and spent extended periods in solitary confinement. I have endured sickness, intense heat, bitter cold, and hunger. I've watched beatings, stabbings, and robberies, I have nearly been in too many fights to count, all of which were avoided only through a divine impartation of restraining grace. In spite of the difficulties, I was able to earn an Associate's Degree in Biblical Studies through the Prison. I study my Bible regularly, enjoy memorizing scripture, and am presently composing an exhaustive theological treatise on the biblical doctrine of death and the afterlife.

I just became a lay leader at the Saturday afternoon worship service and am now living under the best conditions possible at a correctional institution. I always have plenty to eat and no longer suffer the extreme emotional and physical discomfort plaguing my first 3 to 4 years of incarceration. I now hate those things I used to love and love those things I used to hate. I desire holiness and conformity to the image of Christ. I have my heart fixed on attaining wise counsel and on being a positive influence in the lives of those around me. God is teaching me to love all men and to be patient with those who have not yet come to the knowledge of the truth. My patience has been stretched to limits I never thought possible. I've learned to be kind to some of the most intractable, hard-to-love people. I've learned that there are times that I am hard to love too. God has delivered me from drugs, alcohol, to-bacco, a proud heart, a filthy mouth, and all selfish ambition. I now live for the cause of Christ and His everlasting Gospel, to share with others the love and mercy He shared with me. There is no turning back now. Christ owns my soul.

God has already shown me that prison is not the end of my story. In His perfect timing, the Lord will release me into my destiny, for He alone searches hearts and minds. God knows that I never meant for things to happen as they did. However, I understand that although God forgives, this forgiveness does not abrogate the earthly consequences of sin. Thus, I will bear my earthly judgment until the Lord sees fit to release me. Yet I receive much comfort in knowing that these few years of suffering are not even worthy to be compared with the glory that awaits us. It does not matter what we have done in this life. All that matters is what we believe about Jesus Christ: "If we confess our sins, He is faithful and just to forgive us our sins, and to cleanse us from all unrighteousness" (1 John 1:9, NKJV).

Friend, my prayer for you is that you will allow God to build your platform with your pain. He will give you beauty for your ashes and a garment of praise for the spirit of heaviness. We are all going to feel pain in this life. Do not let that pain go to waste. Pain is intended to cure us of our foolishness. Too many of us allow our pain to make us bitter instead of allowing it to serve its true purpose, which is to turn us from ungodly living. I had to learn the hard way what the apostle meant when he wrote, "he who has suffered in the flesh has ceased from sin" (1 Peter 4:1, NKJV).

Sin is only fun for a season. It will take you farther than you want to go, keep you longer than you want to stay, and cost you more than you want to pay. Often we are unable to free ourselves from the iron manacles of sin's power once it takes root in our hearts. Satan has created an enticing world system. It is a system that mercilessly tantalizes, intoxicates, and panders to the depravity of our sinful nature. It is a lie and a deathtrap. There is no good to be gained by engaging in premarital sex, abusing drugs and alcohol, and viewing ribald entertainment. The fleeting pleasures of sin are not worth the untold suffering it will almost certainly bring, both now in this life, and in the life to come. "For the wages of sin is death, but the gift of God is eternal life in Christ Jesus our Lord" (Rom.6:23, NKJV).

"Beloved, do not be deceived. It is the fool who has said in his heart, 'there is no God'"(Ps.14:1). This present world is coming to a sudden and dreadful end. Only those who are willfully blind fail to discern that we are living in the final hour of earth's history. One day soon, the Lord Jesus Christ will split the eastern sky, and what person is then, is what he will always be (Rev.22:11). His holy apostles did not follow cunningly devised fables when they made known to us His power and coming. The good news is that if you are reading this, it's not too late for you. Ask Jesus to manifest Himself to you. He loves you, and He's waiting for you with arms wide open. He will take you as you are. He will never leave you nor forsake you. He gave His life that you might live forever with Him. He will give you a new heart, a new mind, and life more abundantly. You will never be the same. Amen!

— *Jason*

CHAPTER 6

I Was Running From God

My first sin was done in the House of God...

I've been in so much trouble fighting, stealing, and lying.

I remember as far back as five years old. I was going to church with my grandmother, doing church plays and stealing Kool-Aid out of the church kitchen. My first sin was done in the House of God. As I sit here in prison thinking about it, God had a calling on my life. My great-grandfather was a powerful preacher. He and my grandmother were planting spiritual seeds in my life.

I've been in so much trouble fighting, stealing, and lying that I kept running from God like Jonah. In 1986, on September 3rd, I was out doing wrong to myself and others. I should have been at home getting ready for school. I took it upon myself to go out and steal a couple of cars. Before I get started with that, let me tell you how I learned about stealing cars.

My son's uncle took me out with him one night when I was sixteen years old. He asked me if I wanted to make some fast money. I said, "Yes." He took me on the other side of town. First, we started off taking three wheelers and motorbikes. Then, we started going into people's houses, taking food and anything else. Sometimes the people would be at home asleep while we were cooking something to eat and watching TV.

In the midst of my sin, God still kept His mighty hand on me. One night, we went back to a house we had robbed before. Instead of going into the house, this time we went into the garage. There were three safes. One had pennies, the second had silver, and the third one had bills in it. My son's uncle said he wanted all three, so we took the heaviest ones first. On our way out, the garage door slammed closed, so we took the pennies down the hill in back of the house. My son's uncle went back inside, I stayed outside. Something told me to look over at the kitchen window. I saw the curtain move and then saw yellow and blue flames. I used to keep my hat pulled down on top of my head, but I realized I didn't have it on. After seeing the flame, I saw my hat stuck to the garage door. I took off, leaving my son's uncle inside of the garage. Little did I know, he was already out and down the road. There was a hole in the garage. We called for each other and looked for bullet holes. He showed me how to steal a car that night. His words were, "I'm showing you this so that you will always be able to get where you need to be if you are ever lost."

Now back to where I left off at... I was too busy trying to show off since I knew how to steal cars, etc. It was 9:45 p.m. when I left the house. I saw a car with its windows down. Inside was a purse in the driver's seat. I grabbed it and ran. Inside were a few dollars and some food stamps. I made my way down to the night club. After stealing a car, I drove to the other side of town where my son's mother lived. After spending some time with her, I hooked up with her cousin to go steal another car. My son's mother kept asking me to stay with her, but the streets were calling me.

It was Bingo night, and the parking lot was full of cars. I made my move. After taking off, I went back to pick up my cousin and a friend. At this time, it was around 2:45 a.m. We went to make some money with stolen car parts. At the same time, there was a younger man that just left the bar. He was drunk as can be, flying down the street with his headlights off. When we met in the middle, he was going about 75 to 80 mph. I was T-boned on the driver's side. I ended up out of the car and under the vehicle of the drunk driver. The car came to a rolling stop with me under it. Nobody knew where I was including the EMS, Police, and Fire Department. They kept looking. Eventually, the cousin saw my leg sticking out from under the car.

A fireman jacked the car up. I came to and asked him to please get me from under the car. He told me that he couldn't because my neck or my back could be broken. I asked him to come closer until he was within arm's reach. I then grabbed his leg and pulled myself. At the same time, the jack began to slide. The car fell down as soon as I was out from under it.

I was placed in the ambulance, and on my way to the hospital they tried to straighten my leg out. It was broken at the thigh. I was told my feet were pointing at my head. I put on 75 pounds of poison fluid and my mother didn't know who I was. My head was like a medicine ball, and my eyes were deep inside my head. My mother was arguing with everybody at the hospital, telling them that it was not me. She argued with them to the point where she told them to uncover my left leg so she could see my birth mark.

The doctor had to put a tube in my side to help drain the fluid off my lungs. A titanium rod was placed down the middle of my thigh from my hip down to the knee cap. They had to remove the muscle from my upper right shoulder. I had over 12 surgeries, skin graphs, and had to learn how to walk all over again. On September 21, 1986 at 3:00 a.m. in the morning, the man next to me, who had 80-90 percent of his body burned, died. So much happened this day that a nurse named Tim came to me as one of God's angels. He never gave up on me and kept pushing me until I learned to walk again. To this day, I can't find him. There was a little 5 year old girl that came into the hospital. She had pulled hot milk down off the stove, and it dumped on her head, shoulder, and arm.

I remember it so clearly. My family was not coming to see me, and my baby sister visited me more than anybody. I was very hurt, lonely, and in need. God saw what I was going through. Out of nowhere, I heard a baby crying at the top of her lungs. I was being drawn to her. This went on for a few days. One morning I heard her crying again. I got up and went to her. I said, "Hey, what's wrong?" She looked at me and held her arms out, as if asking me to help take her pain away. She was in a metal cage-like bed. From the time she got up until she went to sleep. I was there for her. This was how God took care of my own problems, by helping me learn to be there for somebody else. One morning when I didn't get up, she cried. Neither the nurse nor the doctor was able to get her to stop. They came and got me. The nurse told me I needed to get up because my step daughter wouldn't stop crying.

Each day, we are given a new test to pass. Every test will help us with our problems, only if you put God first. I am sitting in prison with 65 years. Only by the grace of my God and my Lord Jesus Christ am I able to give all this time back. As I stated before, I ran like Jonah for too long. God's plan for my life has taken hold of me. I've been anointed and called to be a minister for God. No more running, I surrender all of me. The question I want to ask you is how long will it take you? I do pray that your eyes will be opened sooner rather than later. Please keep God first.

—*Kool-Aid Guy*

Sin

On page 19, we asked if you had obeyed God's Law.

Have You?

Most people will say, "Yes, I have. I am a good person." Let's focus now and take a close look at some of God's Laws:

Commandment No. 9 says:

You shall not lie.

Have you ever lied? Told a fib? Maybe just a little white lie? Twisted a story to meet your need? Lied when you were a child? Lied at work? Lied on your tax return? Lied for your spouse or kids?

If I lied, what would that make me? A Liar.

Now let's look at Commandment No. 8:

You shall not steal.

Have you ever stolen? Taken something from work? Taken a piece of candy? Cheated on your taxes? Worked for cash and did not claim it as income? In your younger years, did you take anything that did not belong to you?

What is a person called that has admitted to the above? A Thief.

Now let's look at Commandment No. 7:

You shall not commit adultery.

Have you committed adultery? Jesus said, "Anyone who even looks at a woman with lust in his eye has already committed adultery with her in his heart." Have you ever looked at another person with lustful thoughts?

What would a person be called that has done the above? An Adulterer.

At this point we have talked about three of God's Laws. How many have you broken?

Take a moment to go back to page 19. See if you have broken any more of God's Laws.

From here, you can go to the next page and read more "Real Life Stories," or you can skip to page 49 for the next truth.

CHAPTER 7
From Not Knowing God to Leading Worship

Every day my friends and I would get intoxicated or high on drugs...

I was so out of control that I overdosed...

As a young man, I grew up in the inner city of Phoenix, Arizona. Not being raised in a Christian household that taught Christian values, I lived an ungodly lifestyle. My life consisted of running around with friends and experimenting with alcohol, marijuana, cocaine, and other chemical substances. Every day, my friends and I would get intoxicated or high on drugs. I can remember being so out of control that I overdosed after consuming many different drugs at one time. It was by God's grace and mercy that I survived that ordeal. After a bad bout with LSD (acid), I decided to slow down on my chemical consumption and only use marijuana.

At the age of nineteen, I decided to move to Indianapolis to get away from my old neighborhood and those who I associated with on a daily basis. I though by moving away, I could start my life over and rid myself of old habits. Little did I know that Satan had a greater trap waiting for me in a new city. When you are ignorant of Satan's devices, he can further trap you in his web. John 10:10 says, "The thief cometh not, but for to steal, and to kill, and to destroy..."

About six months after being in Indianapolis, my older sister introduced me to a man who was the pastor of a church. After we were introduced, he began to describe certain events in my past that I hadn't revealed to anyone. I became very intrigued at his ability to "see into my past." The following Sunday, I attended the morning and afternoon services. Each service was different. The morning service was like any ordinary church service, but the afternoon service consisted of fortune-telling or reading the congregants minds. Those members that had the ability to read minds would walk through the congregation predicting future events that were to occur in certain members. lives. The afternoon service was like none I had ever seen before.

Soon after, the pastor asked me if I wanted a job driving for him. If accepted, he would teach me how to read minds. The thought of being able to read someone else's mind really excited me. So, I accepted the job. By not knowing much about the Word of God, I had no idea what I was saying yes to. The enemy had successfully pulled me into his trap. As a result of accepting the job, I was given the opportunity to participate in the mindreading classes held at his house twice a week and the séance session once a month. He provided me with material on how to develop your third eye and countless meditation books on how to see into the future. Also, I would sit in on the mindreading sessions he held with clientele across the country. As I developed the method of fortune-telling, I was able to assist him with giving clients readings. Sometimes, he would leave them different types of potions to dispel or attract certain people.

My sister who had introduced me to this minister happened to be visiting a Church one Sunday and gave her life to the Lord. From that point on she began witnessing to me about the Lord and letting me know that I was participating in devil worship. She insisted that I leave the mindreading and séances alone because God was not pleased with my participation in it. One evening my girlfriend and I decided to attend a young couples' service at a Pentecostal church. When the alter call was made, we repented of our sins, were baptized in Jesus name, and were filled with the Holy Ghost. Immediately after receiving the Holy Spirit, God revealed to me that the fortune-telling and calling up the dead were straight from the pits of hell.

I went to see the minister and told him that I could no longer drive for him or attend more services because the Lord had truly saved me. God revealed to me that what I was involved in was not holy. I will never forget the look on the minister's face. It seemed as though God gave me the gift of discernment because I could discern the presence of evil in the minister's countenance. I was finally delivered from the power of darkness because the Son of God had made me free. John 8:36 says, "If the Son therefore shall make you free, ye shall be free indeed."

From that point, I began to attend church on a regular basis. The Lord was blessing me tremendously. By this time, I was twenty-three years old and had found a beautiful wife who loved the Lord as much as I did. My daughter from a previous relationship was now living with us, but, she was having difficulty accepting her step-mother. The enemy was creating problems in my marriage because my daughter could not accept my wife as a mother figure. I became the sounding board for each of them. I had to seek counseling from my current pastor and other married couples who had had similar experiences. It seemed like there was not any peace in the home, and my patience was dwindling away. Eventually, my wife and I started missing church services. We were not praying as much as we used to. Before I knew it, I had backslidden. Satan had stolen my joy and peace in the Lord. I had moved away from the hope of the gospel. I was like a dog that had returned to his own vomit. If I had been more grounded in the faith, I could have easily defeated the enemy of my soul. Since I was up under a strong ministry, I should not have let the enemy steal my joy and peace. It is the duty of Christians, who have sat under the preaching of the gospel, to be well settled in the doctrine of faith, which they have heard and received, and that the best way to be settled, is to be well grounded.

I had become like the prodigal son in the hog pen and went back to some of my old habits, which led to me coming to prison with a seventy-year sentence. Once again, drugs and alcohol use had caused me to do some things that were against the will of God. So God had allowed me to come to prison to come to myself. A few years after being here, I decided to rededicate my life to the Lord. Since coming back to the Lord, my life has changed drastically. I have not used drugs or alcohol in sixteen years. The Lord has used me as a worship leader in the Christian Church in a state prison. I attend prayer meetings in the housing unit where I am presently assigned. Each day, I look forward to how the Lord is going to use me for His glory. I am excited about building the Kingdom of God. I now know that by the Holy Spirit I've got dominion over this flesh. I can do all things through Christ who strengthens me. Because of my past experiences with drugs, alcohol, witchcraft, and marriage, I am allowing the Lord to use me to bring deliverance to those the enemy has in his clutches. Praise be to the Lord!

— N.F.

CHAPTER 8
29 Years Old, Serving
A 30 Year Sentence

Most of my life, I didn't believe in God.

I never thought I needed him....

I am 29 years old, serving a 30 year sentence for selling drugs. For most of my life, I didn't believe in God. I never thought I needed him. The only time I turned to God was when I was in trouble. Then it was only in hopes of getting myself out of the bind I was in.

When I was 18 years old, I had everything a man would want in life, a good job, beautiful wife, son on the way, and family that loved me. Something was missing, and I wasn't satisfied. I started selling drugs. I also had been doing drugs. This started a downward spiral that landed me in prison.

After my wife left me, I got together with my old high school sweetheart, and she had a baby girl. My daughter was the most beautiful thing in the world. A lot of drinking and drugs in a Godless life soon took its toll. An incident with a 12 gauge shotgun took place, and I was on the run. When they got me, I was charged with everything from aggravated assault to drug possession.

In a county jail, I was baptized and prayed daily. They offered me 70 years! When I signed for my time, I stopped praying and said it was a good lawyer that got me five years.

While in prison, I joined a gang. All we did was talk about getting out and selling drugs. We were going to be rich!

I was released from prison May 1, 2006 and quickly started selling meth. My gang gave me rank for the first time, and I felt like I was somebody important. Less than six months later, on October 17, 2006, I got busted.

Here I go, praying again! I ended up with two years and went back on a violation! That's the good lawyer again, right?

Back in prison, I devoted all my time to the gang. I rose to the top and brought a lot of attention to myself! They confirmed me and locked me up in seg. I wasn't worried about it because I was long way discharging. I couldn't wait to take this all to the free world.

January 19, 2010, I was free and clear, with no parole to answer to or anything. I was a high- ranking gang member with plans! My family tried to help me. My son was seven years old. I didn't have time for them. God was definitely not part of my life. I didn't believe in God.

There was nothing holding me back now, so I started selling meth. I was even cooking it. I was shooting up as well. There were plenty of drugs and money. I had the females from our gang hanging around, and when one moved on another moved in. People in the gang were starting to hold their hand out. I was expected to help my "bro's." I was greedy and was not making many friends. Feelings became involved with certain females, and that caused problems too! The gang was turning on me fast. July 2010, I laid it down.

Now, I was on my own. Things started happening that opened my eyes. Being in prison and part of a "white gang," I had been taught to hate. My choices were made for me.

At one point, I was in one town and on the way to another. My girlfriend had to be in court. I was out of gas and had no food, no smokes, nothing. I was standing in front of a convenience store, asking every white person who walked by for help. You would have thought I had the plague! Finally, a black man walked up to me and asked if I was okay. I told him what was going on. He put $20.00 gas in my car, gave me a pack of smokes, and bought us something to eat! Here I was, WHITE, in a tank top, prison tats showing, and a black man helped me. All he said was, "God bless you!" When I turned to thank him, he was driving away! This really made me think.

I got pretty strung out, sticking a needle in my arm six times a day. I did a lot of things I'm not proud of. April 28, 2011, my little stretch ended. I was locked back up, looking at a lot of time.

I went to church and my friend Junior was preaching. Everything he said seemed to be aimed at me. I broke down in tears and begged God to forgive me. This was in May, 2011. I asked God to come into my life.

An old friend came back into my life, and she has helped me more than she could ever know. I made amends with my family, and I am happy. I know with God in my life, I will have another shot at life. I plan on going into the ministry and helping others. If I can do it, anyone can. I come up for parole in October 2014. I know when I get out, this time I can make it because God has changed me.

— *Daniel*

CHAPTER 9
My Desire For All Those Poisons Is Gone

Tragedy befell our family...

My oldest sister died in a car accident...

In 1971, tragedy befell our family. My oldest sister died in a car accident. Kathy and I spent a lot of time together. She took care of me when mom was working, so this created a special bond between us. I was six years old when she was taken from us.

God in his infinite wisdom, sent to my bedside an angel in the form of my sister. The angel spoke reassuring words, telling me everything was going to be alright. God not only brought me comfort, but through me telling the story he also gave comfort to my mom. This was the beginning of a series of incidents during which God was present, but my understanding was minimal.

Several other incidents happened in rapid succession after Kathy's death. I nearly choked to death on cinnamon disk candies. My mom was near by and saved me. I had my ear torn off by a feral cat, and a skilled surgeon reattached it. I fell thirty feet from a tree, landing near an old car chassis, walking away without a scratch. The most prominent incident during this time period was when I nearly drown. The whole family went to visit my aunts, uncles, and cousins. All of us kids decided to go to the swimming hole. I was somewhere around seven years old and fearless. I waded out to the roped off area, not realizing that it was well over my head. I became tired and could not swim anymore, yelling out just before I went under. As I floated to the bottom, I remember being totally at peace. I awoke to see everyone standing over me, all the while hacking up a gallon of water.

My life became peaceful and was calm for many years after this series of incidents. I continued to do normal kid stuff, being involved with my youth group at church, riding dirt bikes, and even racing hydro-plane boats. My childhood was extremely blessed, and looking back I can see how much so.

Dad had always instilled work ethics into us kids. He would tell us we needed to work in order to pay for all of our expensive play toys, like motorcycles, cars, and racing equipment. I started by sweeping the shop floor at the ripe old age of ten. I was operating screw machines at age twelve, making minimum wage of two dollars and thirty five cents an hour. The reason I mention this is because my love of money and the need for more grew from this point on.

In my teenage years, I went to school full time and I also worked. During summer breaks, I would work two full time jobs, putting money away. My senior year I barely squeaked by and graduated. It wasn't because I couldn't do the work but because I had lost interest. Working two jobs, bringing in eight hundred dollars a week, along with cars and women, what more could an eighteen year old ask for in 1984!

This time period in my life directly relates to my use of recreational drugs. It was the mid-eighties. With two of my friends from school, I opened a video arcade. Initially this was fun and exciting, but it quickly started to tax my personal relationships. It also accelerated my drug use.

Cocaine, marijuana, and LSD all were drugs that I took a liking to. I used marijuana to relax, LSD to laugh, and cocaine to keep me going. The drugs became more frequent and were no longer recreational. I was relying on them to get me through the day. This became an expensive habit and a vicious circle working two jobs just to pay for my drug use. Eventually, sometime in the late eighties, I found methamphetamine.

Methamphetamine easily takes over ones life, without the person even realizing it. Chasing the "Meth" high over a couple of decades made me paranoid, angry, and poor. I became a liar, cheat, and thief. I lost three homes, a couple of businesses, and respect from a lot of people. Never does anyone ever grow up and say, "I want to become a meth addict," but it happens. The addiction drew me into situations where I could have very easily been put in a life or death situation. All the while God had his hand on me.

Eventually, I ended up doing some time for a possession charge. The prison time was actually good for me in many ways. It gave me time to get clean and reflect on my life. I could definitely see from this perspective how my life was out of control. When I was released I decided I was going to turn my life around, but the problem was I thought I could do it alone. I did well for a couple of years, but then it happened. I slipped up one time and sank lower than ever. I was ingesting one quarter ounce a day and learning to manufacture this powdered poison.

I finally decided I needed help, laying in my bed after being awake for nearly two weeks. I called out to God to take my addictions from me. I asked Him to please save me from myself and the poisons I continually ingested. A week later, I was arrested. In God's infinite wisdom, He not only saved me from self-destruction but removed the desire for meth and cigarettes!

My incarceration has not stopped the opportunities to get high. As a matter of fact, there has been ample opportunity to even try "new to me" drugs like heroin. Because of my deliverance from addiction, my desire for all those poisons are gone.

I must mention the two most important events in my life. After our twin sons being still born and being told we could not have children,

God had the final say. July 20, 2001 our first daughter, Hope was born. January 10, 2003 Faith was born. Never before have I seen such a miracle or felt so close to God and his creation. Words can not describe the joy and wonder.

The accumulation of our life experiences make us who we are. It forms our personalities and our spirituality. This being said, would I change things if I could? The answer is no because changing those experiences may have made life easier, but it may have also changed my relationship with God. Who am I to resist God's path? At this point in my life, my relationship with Him is better than ever. I hope to continue my spiritual growth through the rest of my days here on the earth.

— *M.W.*

Penalty For Sin

One day, every man, woman, and child that ever lived will have to pay the price for their sins.

The Bible says:

"For the wages of sin is death."   Romans 6:23

Death, meaning eternally (forever) separated from God. Every person will spend eternity somewhere. Heaven or Hell. (There is no in between.) You are either with God or the Devil.

The Bible says:

Then the devil who had betrayed them will again be thrown into the lake of fire burning with sulphur where the creature and false prophet are, and they will be tormented day and night forever and ever.
Revelation 20:10

The Bible also says:

... the corrupt, and murderers, and the immoral, and those conversing with demons, and idol worshipers and all liars — their doom is in the lake that burns with fire and sulphur. This is the second death.
Revelation 21:8

Now, remember your earlier answers to the questions about lying? The Bible says clearly that all liars will be thrown into the Lake of Fire.

At this point, you may be thinking this is hopeless. "I can not obey God's Law." The truth is you can not do it on your own. You need help. God does not want you to face the Fires of Hell and the curse of the Law, and He has provided for you one, and only one chance of escape.

At this point you can go to the next page to read more "Real Life Stories" or turn to page 68 for the next truth.

CHAPTER 10
God's Grace Through
A Life Of Hardship

What is the purpose of life? Some find it hard to answer this question. Through life we experience lots of highs and lows, but is there meaning behind these experiences? Is it possible that we can triumph in victory and defeat? Fasten your seat belts because I am getting ready to take you on quite a journey. I am honored to share my life with you. Though I am only twenty-five years old, I have been blessed in experiencing great highs in life. Moreover, I have been humbled by ignominious falls. At an early age, I discovered that I was gifted athletically. As a result, I got an early start in sports.

I started playing football at the age of seven. On my ninth birthday, my family and I moved to Illinois. It was when we moved that I realized I had a God-given talent in playing the game of football. I played five full seasons with a youth football team. In all of those seasons, I excelled on the field. Football was my love, but I also excelled in other sports. From sixth through eighth grade, I wrestled for a powerful wrestling club. In each of my three seasons in the wrestling club, I earned all-state honors.

In August of 2000, I started high school and had a very successful first year. My sophomore year is when the excitement really began. That season, I ended up being the only sophomore starter on the varsity football team. My sophomore season was the catalyst that propelled me to national prominence. I experienced success my sophomore wresting season, qualifying for the state tournament (the only sophomore in my weight class to do so). Things really began to intensify athletically as I entered into my junior year. As a junior, I was named by a sports magazine as a top junior football player in the nation. In wrestling, I finished sixth in the state at 215 lbs. I had a successful junior year and by the end of my junior year, I had roughly twenty-five written scholarship offers.

After my senior football season, I was named a top star by magazines and football ranking organizations. That was only football though. I still had a wrestling season to tend too, and my goal was to be a state champion. I had a great wrestling season. I won my first thirty-five matches before I lost the only match I would lose. I finished the season third in the state with 36 wins and 1 loss. After the wrestling season, I signed a national letter of intent to attend college on a full football scholarship.

Unfortunately, coming out of high school, I had trouble passing my ACT college entrance exam. As a result, I was unable to qualify academically to attend the college who offered me the scholarship. Eventually, I signed up to take the ACT exam again. If I could pass the test, I would be able to start school in January, 2005. When the time came, I took and passed the exam. Fortunately, because of my status as a standout recruit, I was able to attend a different university. In January of 2005, I enrolled in another college.

Up until this point, most might say I had a good life. Most would say I was the prototypical student-athlete. Regrettably, this was not true. Most did not know that I lived a double life. There was me, the outstanding student-athlete, then there was me, the deceiver, liar, thief, fornicator, cheater, drug abuser, heartbreaker, and most of all the lost soul!

My life up until about age twelve was innocent. I was not a perfect child, but I would say I had a normal upbringing and development. In seventh grade, I became sexually active, although I was yet to lose my virginity. I lost my virginity at the age of fourteen. In retrospect, I am convinced that being involved in sexual activity at such an early age opened the door to sexual intercourse. At the time. I did not realize that becoming sexually involved at such a young age would hinder my development emotionally and cause me not to respect women. All through my teenage years, I broke the hearts of various young women.

At the time, I thought it was cool to be a "player." My attitude was not just destructive to those I hurt, but it also hurt me. I had a beautiful girlfriend throughout my high-school years. She was beautiful in every regard and regrettably, I found a way to hurt her. I was unfaithful to her and when she found out, she broke up with me not knowing she was pregnant. My selfish act devastated her, and she had an abortion without my knowledge or consent. This was the "me" that only a few knew about, but this was not the only aspect of who I was that was destructive.

At the age of thirteen, I began smoking cigars. This habit opened the door to marijuana. I began smoking "weed" at the age of fifteen, and this drug confounded my life. At the time, I thought I could smoke week and still be the best at everything athletically. Because of my lifestyle, I became very prideful. My pride influenced my actions. In reality, all I did was sabotage my own success. My smoking habit not only affected my athletics, it also overwhelmed my personal life. If I did not have marijuana, I would be irritable and would take from anyone to get it. I became less interested in my schoolwork, and my grades began to suffer. Smoking did not just affect me negatively. It was hurtful to those around me.

I had a completely rebellious and hidden lifestyle that not many people knew about. I was sexually promiscuous, I smoked, I drank, I stole, I cheated, and I lied. To be frank, I was not a good person. I had everyone deceived. I deceived the universities and their coaches, I deceived those in my community, I deceived my family to an extent, and I deceived myself the most. I took this destructive lifestyle to college with the thought that I could just continue to scheme my way by as usual. Disappointingly, the joke was on me. I was the most deceived of all, and I was on the highway to destruction.

I arrived on the college campus in Indiana in January, 2005. When I got there, it was the same old behavior; the smoking, the drinking, the lying, the stealing, and the womanizing. I began to discover that it was a bit more difficult keeping the my hidden lifestyle undetected than in the past. In spite of my destructive conduct, I still stood out on the football field. I just happened to be the highest rated recruit that this coaching staff had ever signed. I lived up to the hype, becoming the best freshman on the team. My defensive coordinator told me that if I kept it up I could be one of the best linebackers they ever had. I played in every game I participated in, and I took over the starting position the week of a very important game. It was certain, almost an absolute, that in three to four years I would become a first round draft pick in the NFL! I was on my way, but that secretive life became more and more difficult to conceal. While I was on the football team, I failed at least four to five drug tests due to marijuana. It became harder trying to keep up with my schoolwork, and my grades began to fall. Then tragedy struck! My lifestyle came back and crushed me. I got myself into an overwhelming about of legal trouble. I was arrested, tried before a jury, and sentenced to thirty-seven years in prison. I took an unimaginable fall, and there I lay at the lowest point in my life.

I faced a decision to both stay down and languish in my sorrow, or I could somehow pick up the pieces. I just did not know how to pick up those pieces. What did I have left? After my incarceration, I came to the realization that I had to give up my destructive lifestyle. I was a person who was exposed. When I ran into the legal system, I lost everything. I lost my scholarship, reputation, honor, respect, and my freedom. In a way, I lost my identity. As unusual as this may sound this would turn out to be the best thing that ever happened to me. My whole life was a lie, and when I was exposed, I could not hide who I truly was. Consequently, I forced myself to look in the mirror and change who I was at the very core of my being.

When I came to this point in my life I decided to surrender, and I gave my life to Jesus Christ. I was raised in the church my whole life, but I had a coattail type of faith. I use the word coattail because my faith was not personal. It was based on my parents' faith and their demands that I attend church. I chose to live my life my way, and this led to destruction. However, through this experience, my heart opened to the love of God. I accepted Jesus into my heart February 18, 2006. My life has not been the same since. God has taken my old broken man and shaped me into a true child of his. This is what I want to be properly conveyed. I could never change who and what I was on my own accord. Only God could. I am not claiming to be perfect, but my heart has changed through the grace of God. I am no longer living a lie and all the glory and praise is due to God for his brilliant life-changing work.

I have shared my life because I want to expose the deceptions of this world. In retrospect, we see a young man who has been to the top and was devastated by disreputable falls from glory. I sincerely hope that you understand there is meaning to this thing we call life. I opened with the question of what is the purpose of life, and I am here to tell you that life is a God-given gift to be used for his glory and lived for the betterment of humankind. Through life, we will experience a plethora of highs and lows. It does not matter how many times you fall, as long as you get up every time. Oftentimes, God will use the adverse times in our lives to shape us into the people he intends us to be. It is our responsibility to know that not only do we triumph in victory, we can also triumph when we fall if we respond in a Godly way. With adversity comes opportunity to become triumphant in Christ! Thank you, and God Bless.

— *K.W.*

CHAPTER 11
I Was On The FBI's 10 Most Wanted List

I was just 13 years old when I began stealing hub caps with my friends.

By the time I was 15 years old, I was stealing the whole car.

By the age of 21, I was an enforcer for organized crime.

By the age of 29, I was a bank robber, heroin addict, and next in line for the FBI's 10 Most Wanted List.

My life would be a strange one for a man whose mother had given him to God when he was still a tot in diapers.

When I was eight years old, my Dad came home from the service. Mom had worked as a nurse's aide at the local hospital. With both parents gone, Johnny (my big brother) and I were alone together constantly. He became my best friend, teacher, and father figure. When we were separated, the first seeds of rebellion took root in the fertile soil of anger and hurt.

I stood on the steps of the school one sunny afternoon waiting for Johnny to pick me up. When I opened the door, I saw that he was crying. Silently, I slipped onto the seat beside him and watched the tears rolling down his cheeks. "I have to go with Dad. You're staying with Mom." Dad had divorced Mom, Johnny explained, but they hadn't separated us. That was the judge's decision. A judge was somebody who sentenced murderers to the electric chair and made bad men go to prison. Why would a judge want to take Johnny away from me? Johnny took me home, but this was the last time. I stood on the sidewalk crying as I watched his car vanish around the corner.

At first, I couldn't accept the fact that one man, a judge, could have the power to separate Johnny and me. All I knew was that the judge had torn my young life apart. He was against me. He wanted to destroy me. He hated me – so I hated him back with an anger I had never known before.

Mom and Dad still went to the same church. Church, I decided, was an uncomfortable place. Sitting in church meant being hurt. So I started sneaking out. Praying could go on half the night. That gave some of us kids plenty of time to find something fun to do. No one would notice a couple of skinny boys slipping down the aisle. Since it was a Pentecostal church, everyone had their hands raised and eyes closed. We slipped out and met in the parking lot behind the church. The first night, we stuck to the church grounds. The second night, we got up enough nerve to go down to the amusement park two blocks away. It was exciting and harmless enough, except for one thing – I didn't have enough money. The quarter that Mom had given me for the offering plate didn't go very far in the park.

The next week, all my friends, except me, backed out. They decided that sooner or later they'd get into trouble, but that didn't bother me. If Mom wanted to waste half the night in church, fine. I was going to the park. One Sunday night, the inevitable happened. I didn't make it back to church in time, and I found Mom waiting in the parking lot for me. What did she do? She prayed. Mom was one of those "prayer warriors" who figured that the solution to every problem was prayer – hard prayer.

I didn't need anyone praying for me, and I didn't want God or anybody else to change me. For years, I flew into a rage whenever anyone said they were praying for me.

Soon after my church friends chickened out, the two of us who were still going to the park found some new friends who wouldn't chicken out. They didn't go to the church. One of the boys, Jim, a freckled-face red head with an Irish temper, had been friends with me since elementary school. Years later, we would still be friends – as partners in organized crime and one of the most dangerous teams in the mid-west. But for now, we were just a couple of kids trying to pick up a buck or two. When we stole our first set of hub caps, it was just for a prank. A man approached us to ask if the hub caps were for sale. We accepted his offer eagerly. The man told us he wouldn't mind having a few more hub caps. He'd even like a few "extras" too . . . and he'd pay a lot more. For the next few months, we stole hub caps and "extras." Within two years, we had graduated to wholesale car theft. We stole cars, stripped them, and sold the parts to the man in the park and some other men.

When I entered high school, I discovered a talent that would become my career – violence. I had always been a good fighter because Johnny and his friends were six years older than me. I had always had a mean streak, too. When I was just six years old, I put our paperboy in the hospital. Every day, the paperboy would try to hit me with our paper. One day when I saw him coming, I dragged a snow shovel behind a tree. When he rode by, I jumped out and swung the shovel with all my might. The bike went in one direction, the boy went in another, and papers flew all over the street. Everyone thought that I hadn't really meant to hurt him, but they were wrong. I wasn't sorry at all when the ambulance came. Now I was in high school. I was bigger and meaner. One day a guy stabbed me in the knee, and I threw him down a flight of concrete stairs. He landed at the bottom, right in front of a door just as the teacher was stepping out into the hall. I got expelled. I didn't think it was fair, but then I knew the authorities never were fair. I got expelled again when a teacher hit me on the hand with his stick for having a comic book hidden in my math workbook. He meant to knock the book out of my hand, but he missed and came down on my knuckles. I reacted on instinct – I jumped up and slugged him.

I graduated from high school. It was the 1950's, the era of the leather jackets, duck tails and motorcycle gangs. I had it all. I had already made up my mind what I wanted to be. My hero was the James

Cagney type gangster. I wanted to be just like him – a top gangster, not just a thug.

"You got the right temperament," a rough-looking sergeant barked at me. He made me squad leader two weeks after I arrived at the Air Force Base. By "the right temperament," he meant that I was as mean as a snake. I started fighting almost the minute I arrived and didn't stop for three years.

After basic training, I was shipped to an Air Force Base in Germany. I hadn't been in Germany but a few days before I discovered that the little frauleins were only too willing to play all kinds of games with the American soldiers. I began a lucrative business in prostitution. I soon got involved in a host of black market activities and was making money hand over fist. I was having a great time. I played drums in the base band, wrecked cars for guys who wanted to collect the insurance money, raced, gambled, and as always – fought. I had a summary court martial for my "attitude", and was always in one kind of trouble or another.

(Many incidents in the military contributed to my ability to have to deal with physical pain which planted seeds of drug addiction.) I was discharged from the hospital and the Air Force on the same day, in February, 1958. I had no plans, but I decided to go back to Indiana and find something, perhaps around Chicago. That night, I pumped myself full of pills to make the drive from Philadelphia to Indiana without stopping. I'd be home by morning.

As it turned out, I wouldn't be home for another year. On a sudden whim, I decided to stop for a quick drink at a bar I knew. When I went in and sat down, a middle-aged man who introduced himself as Tony struck up a conversation with me about his son who was still in the service. Soon, he was buying my drinks and telling me how much I reminded him of his son. A couple of hours later, he invited me for a night on the town. "All the drinks on me!" he urged.

"Come on – you can leave in the morning." "Why not?" I thought to myself, "If he's got the money, I guess I can make the time."

As soon as we sat down at the first bar, the bartender walked over to us and slipped Tony a white envelope. I didn't think anything of it until it happened again … and again. I wondered about it but didn't want to ask questions. When we walked into the fifth bar, again the bartender came up to us. This one started yelling and cursing Tony then suddenly slugged him. Before I knew it, I had landed on the bartender and worked him over. When I straightened up my tie and returned to Tony, I noticed he was looking at me in a new light. He was grinning from ear to ear.

That night, Tony hired me as an enforcer for his organized crime operations. I was ready for the job, and I wanted the money. My career was on the up. I was getting paid for doing what I always did for free. I rarely went to a bar without hurting somebody before the night was over anyway.

A few weeks into my career, I was sent to a club in Wildwood, New Jersey to do some enforcement. I ended up doing too much. The manager wasn't cooperating. I got mad, started punching, and just went crazy. I busted his shoulder with the butt end of the double barreled shotgun I used and then shot up the place. The club looked like a tornado had hit it. When I walked out, the manager was lying on the floor groaning.

The incident was a turning point in my career. It gave me a reputation, which is almost as valuable as a gun in enforcement. The brutality of the incident alarmed the local police and suddenly I was the "dangerous new man" to East Coast crime operations. Across the nation, law enforcement agencies that kept tabs on organized crime activities sat up and took notice.

A few weeks later, I was in a club, as a client, when I overheard a man at the next table talking about some enforcer. "And you should have seen the club when 'Happy Jack' got through with it!" When he mentioned where the club was located, I realized he was talking about me. I had been nicknamed "Happy Jack" by some friends because I snickered during an act of enforcement. I liked the name, and it stuck! I was happy.

When I was in a bad mood, which was almost all the time, I would punch some poor guy for no reason. I would wind up in court the next day. Violence was my way of relieving frustration. After I would punch some guy who had done nothing to me but honk his horn or get in my way, I'd get a phone call the next morning. "Jack," my lawyer would sigh, "We have another assault and battery charge against you." I'd go into court, pay the fine, and walk out. We both got tired of the routine, and it was costing me a lot of money. So, I put an end to it. When he told me that someone had filed an assault and battery charge against me, I would find out who was filing it, go to his house and tell him to go down to court and drop the charges or he'd be hurt a lot worse next time. The charges were always dropped.

There were so many incidences of violence I was responsible for... and I'm now certain God wasn't laughing. A nice old Salvation Army man came by my cigar store every week to collect donations from my customers. One week when he came in, I was annoyed and threw a $10 bill in his hat just to hurry him up. I didn't want my customers bothered with religion. When the old man saw the bill, he exclaimed gratefully, "Why, son, God bless you! I'll be praying for you ..." "Son, I'm praying for you ... God promised and I'm praying for you ..." Mom's words always brought back a flood of emotions. I felt the anger rise up inside. I hit the old man, picked him, up and threw him out the door.

Just about every law enforcement agency in various parts of the country was trying to come up with enough evidence to send me off to prison for life. Staying one step ahead of the law was a thrill for me all of its own. However, my luck staying one step ahead of the law eventually ran out. Four days after my arrest, I was handed a letter through the bars. It was from my wife, Carolyn. I sat down on my cot and began to read. I wasn't prepared for this:

"I have given up all hope for you. I have prayed for you for seven years, but now I know that not even God could reach that far down in the gutter ... not even God could change a man like you. I know that you will be out soon, but I don't want you to see me or the children again – ever."

At last, all the anger and hurt that my wife had suffered all these years had come out. When Carolyn heard that I had robbed another bank and had been arrested, she couldn't take any more. She was sick of the hurt I had caused her, sick of loneliness and fear. I didn't blame her. She had been faithful to me all these years, she had stayed with me and loved me. As I read the letter again, I realized how much she had loved me to stick it out this long.

I had pushed emotions aside for so many years. I hadn't felt the sting of rejection since I was a child. At first, I was sorry that I had lost my last tie with the outside world. Then I realized the aching in my heart was something deeper. A terrible loneliness swept over me as I sat on the cot staring at the letter. I suddenly realized than no one in the whole world loved me.

I began to long for God to make Himself real to me. Evidently, He determined it was the right time to make His reality known to me personally. I went into the cell, fell on my knees, and cried like a baby. I hadn't cried since I was 11 years old, but now I couldn't stop the tears. My family had called. Carolyn still loved me. God had done this. He had given me back my family, not just the sign I asked for that someday I could have them back. God did love me. Jesus did go to Calvary for me.

I didn't care that 27 other prisoners were standing in the cell watching me. Nothing mattered to me but God. My surroundings fell away, and mentally I was a thousand miles away from the jail. I didn't know how to say a prayer. I remembered that a man had told me to ask Jesus into my heart, and He would wash my sins away.

I couldn't get the words out fast enough. "Jesus," I cried, "I don't know what you can do with this mess I've made of my life, but if You want it, it's Yours. Oh Jesus, come into my heart and make me a new person."

As I wept and prayed, it felt like God reached down and turned a faucet on the inside of me ... and the hate and anger flowed out. The greatest peace I had ever known flooded my heart, and I knew something tremendous was happening to me. I poured out my heart to God – and He was pouring out His heart to me.

After that, God put a bigger, happier smile on my face that many say has never left. The name "Happy Jack" followed me wherever I went, but the reason for being happy wasn't because I took pleasure in hurting people like before. I was now happy knowing God loved me, forgave me, and I was working for the REAL "boss" – THE Judge who controls the eternal destiny of every person.

God graciously released me from prison much sooner than my scheduled sentencing time originally pronounced by the judge. After my spiritual born again conversion, my heart began to have deep concern for other inmates and the families and close friends of those inmates. That concern didn't leave me once I walked outside those prison walls. I had an ever-growing desire to go back into the prisons to help people find peace with their Creator like I had been so blessed to have found. God placed a call on my life and my precious wife Carolyn's life. He opened doors in so many prisons across the country and even out of country that I couldn't begin to count how many we've ministered in.

— *Happy Jack*

CHAPTER 12

Filling the Void

My dad was my hero. All I ever wanted was to please him and receive his validation.

His disappointment was painful, evident to me every time I'd failed.....

I was catching the biggest game of my young life and had made an error earlier that cost us a run. In the top of the 12th inning, tied 5-5, I arrived at the plate with 2 out and a fog rolling in over the outfield fence. I didn't have a hit yet in the game. Having struck-out 4 times, I had been continually admonished by my coach and my dad to shorten my natural power swing and just try to make contact. My dad was my hero. All I ever wanted was to please him and receive his validation. His disappointment was painfully evident to me every time I'd failed in this game.

I stood in the batter's box facing the opposing team's 4th pitcher of the game. He had a nasty curveball, yet I had only one thing in mind, "I'm a power hitter, and I can end this with one swing." After fouling-off 2 fastballs, I moved way up in the box to cut down the effect of the likely oncoming curveball. My dad roared from the stands, "What are you doing?" I didn't even look over this time. I dug in, praying for a curveball. That's just what I got. I took my natural full rip, connecting and sending the ball sailing deep into left-center field. The center fielder raced toward the ball as it disappeared into the fog and over the outfield fence for a homerun. I was mauled as I crossed home plate with the winning run and then carried off the field by my teammates. As I gathered myself, I heard my mom yelling for me, thrilled with the outcome. She lauded praises on me and asked if I needed anything. I asked, "Where's Dad?" She said, "He said he'd see you at home".

I'll never forget that moment and the wound that opened up. A rebellious, misguided spirit was birthed in the fertile ground of a deep void I believed my dad was supposed to fill. We had a very dysfunctional family. The love I experienced was mostly conditional, depending on good grades and success in sports. I did have one close friend my age I could trust. Doug was always there for me no matter what.

The 70's were full of great music, drugs, and pornography. All of these provided an inviting playground for a lost and wounded dreamer. That's exactly what I did: Let's Party! Doug quit drinking and never did like the drugs. Our conversations became spiritually oriented, and the two-faced lives the role models in our lives displayed made us wonder what really mattered.

Doug moved from our town, several hours away. I felt another great void in me. Anything I did now was justified in my eyes, I felt betrayed. Even the very salvation of my eternal soul was now a question for me. Where could I turn?

Towards the end of the summer Doug left, I was able to go visit him. On the phone he'd told me about finding the truth in Jesus and living a Holy Spirit filled life. He warned against my bringing any drugs with me and said he wanted me to meet some friends of his. I went curiously to see him and upon my arrival was shocked to see such a great change in him. Doug had two close friends that stayed overnight with us, staying up late answering my endless questions. Finally, I was frustrated at the prospect of not having a realization of the powerful truth they exhibited, so I asked them to pray for me. We all held hands kneeling, and they interceded on my behalf, ending up with my pleading to God, "If you are real let me know." Boy, did He! (Matthew 7:7)

I got hot from my head to my toes and then freezing cold. Suddenly. I felt a huge hand on my back and that heat rushed over me again.

In a small, still voice I heard, "I'm here!" They led me in a sinner's prayer, and I accepted Jesus as my savior. I had the Holy Spirit now and went home on fire for the Lord.

Unfortunately, I was met with less than an encouraging spirit from family and friends (Matthew 10:34, 35). On the contrary, it seemed as if they had all been laying in wait for me, primed and ready to jump down my throat.

I didn't last long without getting plugged in with a spiritual mentor or a good church. I vowed to tell everyone the truth about Jesus. I just wasn't going to live like I knew it. My life became a continuing spiral of depression and failures, trouble with the law and family, brief stints in county jail, and the cries to God from those cellblocks. My life progressed, and I became older and more experienced at how to avoid the law. God hadn't forgotten His call on my life (Psalm 103:13). He was the Father I needed, but I was rebellious and unwilling to live by the faith He had given me.

I tried a geographical change, joining the Army and getting married. Sparing you the gruesome details, our marriage produced only one lasting beauty, the birth of our son Matthew. I still didn't understand or trust my Father, so how could I begin to be one. After a heart wrenching divorce and going back home a failure, I upped the ante in my drug use. Nothing was off limits, and there was a new way to get high on cocaine I'd yet to experience: smoking it. The first time I tried it I was hooked. The intense euphoric rush it produced was the escape I'd been looking for. Nothing else mattered besides getting and using more. I was cashing bad checks within 2 weeks and pawning everything I owned or could get my hands on. I was out of control. I remember imagining ludicrous scenarios where I'd pay back money I'd stolen from family or friends. They never materialized (Matthew 6:22, 23).

At the end of a long dark road, after a 2 week binge where I drank and used everything I could get my hands on, I woke up in a cornfield across from my parents' house. I had long since been banned from their residence. I walked through the neighborhood in a haze. When I came to the house of an old acquaintance, my only thought was to borrow some money for more dope. When I'd left, a dear old woman I'd worked for and known for years was tied up in her bedroom to ensure my get away. Trying to free herself, she asphyxiated on a gag. Later the next day, I was arrested for murder (Romans 6:23).

In the State Penitentiary, 4 years later, I made a decision to take responsibility for my life. I knew it would be the hardest thing I'd ever attempted, but I didn't want my son to be left with the legacy I'd written thus far. I prayed and cried out from the depths of my soul, "Protect and raise my son and I'll live for you." I started the most rewarding adventure of my life that day, and the Lord has never let me down (Hebrews 13:5).

The void I'd felt so many times before began to fill with the Love of God, at church, at work, in the cell house, and out at recreation, I began to run into serious men of God. They encouraged me, prayed with and for me, gave me food and clothing, and we began studying the Word of God together. My faith increased tremendously (Romans 10:17).

The challenges I faced in the strongholds of my past we met together, and I had a newfound knowledge of my identity in Christ and its corresponding power through God. The blessings of a real and living covenant relationship, by the precious Blood of Jesus, with an all-knowing and all powerful God were active in me now. I knew and loved my true Father, and He was teaching me to be a real man of God. It wasn't easy, and it didn't happen overnight.

I stumbled and fell plenty, yet Jesus was always there to pick me up. I was constantly challenged on my new identity, and in the heat of the moment I sometimes resorted (in pride) to old familiar ways. I learned how to repent and get back in line with God. I fought less with other inmates, and heated confrontations became the exception rather than the norm. I was learning how to walk in love and forgiveness. Humility was the hardest for me early on. Pride had deep roots in me, so the Lord used a near death experience to create a new heart in me. (Psalm 51:10)

I left the Prison bleeding to death early one morning. The word around camp the next day was I had died. In a way, I had. When I arrived at the emergency room, the nurses working on me relayed their amazement that I was conscious to the doctor. I tried to comfort them, encouraging them I'd be all right, blessing them with my open prayers, and thanking God for seeing me through this. Before I'd left the prison, the Lord gave me a promise from His Word. It was (Psalm 91:2).

After receiving over 6 pints of blood transfused into me, I recovered peacefully chained to a hospital bed. Two weeks later I returned to general population at the prison and continue my ministry to the lost and wounded souls here. God has restored my family relations, and I see my prayers answered without fail in their lives. My son Matthew came to see me. After sitting across from me for a few hours he made a statement I'll never forget. He said, "Dad, I never thought I'd be telling you this in prison, but I'm proud of you." At that moment, I felt a load lifted off me I didn't even know was there. A void in both our lives was filled by a gracious and loving Father!

I made a promise to my Lord, that neither His Son's death, nor the victim's would be in vain. He has used me beyond my imagination, here in prison. I have more true peace and real freedom now than ever before (John 14:27).

— C.N.

God's Love

For God loved the world so much, that he gave his only Son, so that anyone who believes in him shall not perish, but have eternal life.

John 3:16

God loved His creation (you) so much that He sent His Son to earth to pay the full price for all sin.

Jesus did not come to the earth to do away with God's law. He came to fulfill it.

Jesus came as a man in the flesh and did not sin. Not one time. He obeyed the commandments, God's Law. Fully. He did for you what you could never do.

Jesus was beaten, tortured, and hung on a cross. While on that cross, the sins of the world (your sins) were placed on His shoulders.

Jesus died for and with your sins, but death could not hold Him; the grave could not contain Him. He arose from that grave paying the full price for every person's sin. (That includes you.)

It is only through God's Love, God's Mercy, and God's Grace that we can escape the curse of the law.

From here, you can go to the next page for more "Real Life Stories," or skip to page 81 for more truth.

CHAPTER 13

A Stepping Stone

The first twenty-seven years of my life was.....

The first twenty-seven years of my life was filled with both materialism and chaos. Growing up in an Indiana home with divorced parents fit the common mold of a dysfunctional family. My father was seldom around because he was always working. I was left at home with my stepmother, whom I could hardly stand to be around. We never quite had that mother/son relationship that every child longs for early in life. I believe this is a crucial period for children to develop values and beliefs from their mother and father. I feel I was a bit behind in the area of guidance as a child, as opposed to some of the other kids I grew up with. I have considered the idea that lack of family relationship is how materialism easily gained a stronghold on me at such a young age and boosted my life into chaos.

My father's quick and rash decision to skip out on his D.W.I. court hearing would prove to be the beginning of a distasteful life for me. Instead of making that short trip downtown to the local courthouse, our family made a several hour journey to the hot sweltering state of Arizona. This is the place where I was first introduced to sex. Sex in itself has proven to gain power over individuals. Just being able to see two people having sex for the very first time can stain an undeveloped mind for many years to come. The majority of the entertainment the secular world enjoys each and every day is centered in and around sex and drugs. Simply watching television is one of the toughest to overcome. I can remember watching movies at a young age that had explicit sex scenes and thought to myself that I was actually learning how to perform sex. I did not learn all the details merely from watching television, but it certainly put my sex drive into overdrive. This motivation only became stronger and stronger.

By the age of twelve, we found our way back to the plains of Indiana where I first began having sex with a serious girlfriend. Having sex, even as young as I was, seemed to be right at the time. I thought to myself, all my friends were doing it. As the years went by, I noticed that television became more sexually explicit. As the obsessions of the world were changing, I felt as if I was being pushed into sexual expectations.

By the age of fourteen, I drifted into the drug scene. Starting with tobacco and alcohol, it progressed into harder drugs and more sexual experiences. Looking back on the matter, I can see just how troubled I truly was. I can remember feeling lonely and lost throughout most of my childhood. This may have been due to little guidance or structure within my family. I pretty much did whatever I wanted, whenever, and with whomever I chose. By the eighth grade, I was doing so poorly in school my coach had no choice but to kick me off the football team. The one thing that is most astonishing to me now is that I thought being kicked off the team was cool at the time. This was a true sign of someone who was not focused or on the right track. I wish there was someone who could have noticed and taken action to help me see my foolishness. There I was, a young boy full of arrogance and pride, thinking I had everything figured out, only to discover how little I really knew.

Now in high school, the sex and drugs perpetuated. It was not long into the first semester that I was skipping classes to use drugs. I did very little homework, but the teachers let me slip on through the tenth grade – somehow. I began dating an older woman and was convinced I had everything going for me. I was too cool for school and family and way too cool for church. There I was, just sixteen, dating a twenty-year-old, who was a mother of one from a previous marriage. Then just before the second year of school ended, "BANG"! We were pregnant.

I promptly quit school and proceeded to become a father. By father,

I mean I decided to maintain a job and live the American dream. Turns out, it was quite harder than expected. Before we knew it, two years had passed and another child had come into our lives. Time quickly passed. Two more years, our third daughter arrived. I was working a dead-end job and looking for the answers to life. Seven years flew by, and during this time my relationship with my wife deteriorated. I lost my family.

By the age of twenty-seven, sex and drugs had finally gotten the best of me. I found myself in a jail cell for the first time in my life. While awaiting trial on multiple sex and drug crimes, it was there my cell-mate introduced me to the word of God. I prayed and talked with him for hours and quickly found that I enjoyed doing so. This was the point in my life when God revealed to me change was ever so important. Little did I know, ten months later I would be sentenced to one-hundred-and-twenty years in a maximum-security prison. I could not believe the words the judge had muttered. A week later, I was in prison. I lack the words to convey just how lonely and scared I felt, shackled in the backseat of a van, as we left my hometown to likely never return. Just when I thought I could not be anymore terrified, we arrived at the state prison. My eyes had never seen such an ugly place. It was not long after my arrival before I decided through prayer and hope that I was going to make the best of this difficult and terrifying situation.

There is a specific Scripture which says, "Ask, and it will be given you; seek, and you will find; knock, and it will be open to you" Mat. 7:7. Oh, how ever true those words are. I will now tell you friend, my hundred and twenty year prison term was cut in half by the court of appeals roughly a year after arriving at the penitentiary. It is dreadfully real to me that I still have a lot of time to serve, but it just goes to show the power God has and what is possible through our persistence in seeking Him.

Growing up in a secular home left me with very little knowledge of God and His word. After I obtained my G.E.D, I promptly made the decision to enroll in the college program within the prison. This would turn out to be the best thing I could have ever done while in-carcerated, since it was Christian based. The instructors were some of the truest people I had ever met, and they had all the knowledge I had been desperately seeking for some time. Over the course of four years, I learned everything from who Christ is and what He wants from me, to principles of management within a business. I not only found myself seeking Jesus Christ through Bible studies in between classes, but I also started reading my Bible at 3:30 a.m., awaiting breakfast lines to start my day. It was not long before I began to find true enjoyment within those brief studying of the Scriptures each morning. I noticed reading the Scriptures early in the day seemed to give me some sort of comfort throughout the course of my day, which gives me positive things to think about.

Now that college is near its end, I intend to keep my mind on the Lord and the things He requires from me. I am determined to draw more people to Christ. Believers can have a huge impact in other lives, even at unexpected times. I certainly hope I can aid in life-changing experiences for others that are here with me. I know I am still a work in progress, but life is better with Christ, even here in prison. With that being said, I am thrilled about the journey that lies ahead and what God has in store for my life. If it had not been for the judge being so tough on me at sentencing, I do not know what state of mind I would be in today. The day I asked Christ to come into my life was the day of my new beginning. God has changed me and freed me from the life of sex and drugs. Friend if you have not asked God to forgive you and for Him to become a part of your life, I cannot begin to explain to you what you are missing. If it is your desire to experience real love and true friendship, this is "necessary" for you. It is my hope this has been a stepping-stone in the right direction.

— M.S.

CHAPTER 14
Poor, Pardoned, and Paroled

Jesus told me I don't need to stare at your pictures anymore.

You can grow up in the church and still not grow close to God...

I was born into a family of poverty on April 15, 1974 in the city of York Pennsylvania. I was the first-born son to two young and struggling parents of my older sister. Named after my father, my life would soon follow what characterized him best, a rolling stone. My mother would bear this man three more children, all of whom were born in different states. We settled in southern Indiana, and shortly thereafter the home was divided in a divorce due to the continued irresponsibility of my father. At this time my struggling young mother joined a local church where we children were to be raised. She remarried several years later and continued in the habit of attending church with her new husband. This relationship would also be defined by frequent moves and moments of uncertainty.

At the age of eight, during a Sunday school class, I came to "recognize" my need for Christ. Although I could not intellectually process this need, I responded to the tug of my heart and accepted Jesus into my life. For many years to come, my life would follow a rollercoaster in my relationship with Christ. Due to the lack of insight and inconsistent spiritual mentoring, I fell away, believing God was angry with me. I began to pursue the world.

Leaving home at sixteen, I chased after women, drugs, and money. I found myself in multiple unhealthy relationships. It was easier to be involved with somebody rather than be left alone with all of the hurt, frustration, and emptiness I felt inside. This emptiness later motivated me to investigate the world of the supernatural. Upon doing so, the door of my heart and life was flung wide open to the powers of darkness. Against my better judgment, I attended séances (contacting the spirit world in an attempt to communicate with the "dead" or other-worldly spirits) and dabbled with the Ouija board.

My soul entered into one of the greatest struggles between light and darkness I thought I would ever face. I grew angry and lashed out at others, despising life and the condition, of my soul. The more I struggled, the more I ran. The more I ran, the deeper into sin I plunged. God continued tugging at my heart and mind, many times, by sending people across my path inviting me to return. But how could I? Why would God want to accept me? After all, I had not found it within me to live up to what I believed was God's requirements. I had tried … and failed. Tried … and failed. My history with God was not very commendable.

Little did I know that as I continued running from God, Satan's intentions for me were much different than I imagined. I never set out to "serve" the devil, yet through my decisions I became a "willing" participant and instrument of his design. At twenty-four I attempted to settle down, fathering three children and marrying a sweet young lady. However, through my instability I grew colder and became more calloused and unfeeling toward family, others, and the world around me. It became easier to use people to arrive at whatever goals I had in mind. Usually, these goals were directed toward instant gratification, as an attempt to ease the pain. I had no forethought of the rippling consequences and the wake of devastation imposed by such abusive actions.. Eventually, it cost me dearly. It's price … the cost of a life. For many, at my young age of twenty-six, the free world turned out to be a better place on the misty morning of July 24, 2000. My sudden disappearance from society, through my arrest, would cause many to rest more peacefully at night. My actions would live on in their memories for some time to come.

Lying in a holding cell, convulsing and vomiting from drug withdrawal, I was left alone, again, agonizing over how I had ended up in such a predicament. In a moment where I felt no hope of the present or future, I felt God massaging my cold heart and sensed His presence. I don't remember how long I cried. But I cried until the tears no longer came as I talked to Him. I don't recall all that I said, but I do remember telling Him that no matter how many years I would face, that I would serve Him for the rest of my life. His love for me was so real. There were no thoughts of Him rejecting me in that moment. However, my recommitment was tested two short years later when I was found guilty and sentenced to ninety-three years for the capital offense of murder and probation violation. My mind swam with thoughts of horror and the possibilities of a future isolated from family, being out of touch with all the things I had known and believed to be true.

After arriving at prison, I struggled angrily for nearly five years trying to "adjust" to this new way of living. During this time, God made His grace available to me as I processed and worked through some of the decisions of my past. One instrument He used was my enrollment in Bible College. This education helped me to study and apply the Bible in a meaningful yet practical way in my present circumstances. It has also helped me to process information and make better informed decisions. Little did I know that God was using this time as training ground.

My relationship with the Church grew. I began feeling the tug of God, just as I had as a child, to minister His Word. Others began to recognize the call of God on my life. I was invited to leadership meetings. I began teaching Bible studies in our living quarters. The responsibility of remaining teachable, while teaching others, is a task I found to be very difficult. I've discovered that when God calls a person into ministry, He does not call them because they're perfect, He perfects them through their calling. These "revelatory" moments were the very catalyst God used to birth messages of hope and truth to those within the sphere of influence I had been appointed to. This sphere of influence grew as I submitted more and more of myself to Him. As Scripture in Luke 16:10-11 indicates, "He who is faithful in a very little thing is faithful also in much; and he who is unrighteous

little thing is unrighteous also in much. Therefore if you
been faithful in the use of unrighteous wealth, who will
he true riches to you?" As God continued opening doors of
opportunity I was challenged, stretched, and pleasantly delighted at
discovering the wealth of potential lying within me. This potential,
of the Holy Spirit, was put into greater action as God stirred my
heart to begin writing articles for the a christian newsletter. Several
years following, the Lord laid it upon my heart to begin a newsletter.
My experience with the previous newsletter proved to be invaluable.
From this, a new newsletter was birthed. What an awesome God!

God continues stretching me as He opens doors for me. This previous year I was called upon to help shepherd the congregation here
at the state prison. It has been a challenging task which has taught
me many things. Among them, it certainly has increased my appreciation and understanding of what many ministers and pastors
face. This newfound appreciation has enabled me to pray more ef-
fectively for those in the field of ministry. It has, thus far, been an
awesome journey of which I have faced plenty of doubt and moments of great uncertainty, yet God has proven faithful. My life is
truly in His hands, and He has promised to return for me.

Perhaps as you read this you have resigned yourself to believing
that God could not or would not do the same with you. My friend,
I assure you the enemy wants you to believe this lie. You are more
valuable to God than you can image. Whatever it is that you're looking for can only be found in Him. He needs you. Yes, I said it, "God
needs you!" He needs you to be His eyes, His ears, His hands, His
feet, and His voice to the world around you. "... God hath chosen
the foolish things of the world to confound the wise; and God hath
chosen the weak things of the world to confound the things which
are mighty; And base things of the world, and things which are despised, hath God chosen, yea, and things which are not, to bring to
nought things that are: That no flesh should glory in his presence.
But of him are ye in Christ Jesus, who of God is made unto us wisdom, and righteousness, and sanctification, and redemption: That,
according as it is written, He that glorieth, let him glory in the Lord"

(1 Cor. 1:27-31). Through being an instrument of His handiwork, Grace is imparted, lives are changed, and He receives all the Glory. Your yesterdays do not have to define you and limit your present circumstances. Where God is, He will make a way.

Finally, all the years of my mother and friends praying for me are being realized. It is, to a certain degree, a tragedy that it took these circumstances. Where I was spiritually poor, blind, naked and really ashamed, today, I have been pardoned, and forgiven from all past, present, or future sin, through the shed blood of Christ. He has paroled me, releasing me of the awful debt of the past. I now have true freedom. The freedom to truly love, to truly serve, to truly smile, and to truly be the person God has made me within this universe and time on earth. You can have the same thing. How bad do you want it?

— *D.K.*

CHAPTER 15
The Gutter-Most
To The Uttermost

On May 28, 1966, the world I knew as a young kid from the streets of Gary, Indiana ended. I was taken into custody by the probation officer. To be delivered up is a lonely state. I was charged with a capital offense and experienced the loneliest night of my life. I was delivered up again, to be taken into custody by the Sheriff.

As the sounds of Gary faded in the background, the sound of "rescue me" resonated outside the squad car. My life drastically changed as I was taken to jail. I was placed in the criminal section where the worst of the worst are placed. Growing up was an overnight requirement. When you are thrown into the arena you will be tested, gorged, eaten, beaten, or killed. The law of the jungle demands nothing less. As a kid, I always had the security of my big brother. Realization clearly mandated instant decisions. I had the guidance of some decent men who recognized the heart of a champion beating within me.

Years later I learned the road map is predestined. The prayers of the Saints were working for my good. Before the year was out, I was sentenced to 10 – 25 years in prison. I cut my teeth on steel and concrete. I was now ready to be delivered up again. It seemed the long drive to State Reformatory, went much faster than expected. Before I knew it, the Sheriff Deputies were turning me over to the charge of the superintendent. I was then taken to G-cell house Quarantine Section, after leaving the Round House – dress out – haircut – delousing – degradation – humiliation and the catcall fish line walk to 2 weeks of orientation. One thing about the whirlwind adjustment period for the last seven months is that it readied every fiber and sinew of my being. Then, a fool was born. Larry died, and Truck – T Man – Mack Truck extraordinaire was born.

In spite of all this, I was blessed to receive a time cut for erroneous sentencing. I was home in a heartbeat. The reputation of Truck had preceded my arrival. Needless to say, many post-graduates of the prison system had come through and touched base with me. Then in 1975 on Valentine's Day, I was delivered up again. This time the full effect of the law was metered out to "Truck," and I was not going anywhere until I came to myself. Entering the state prison I was determined to do just what the Judge had said ... life. The genie was out of the bottle and was never going to see freedom, so I developed an attitude of worst case scenario. After weighing the options I determined I was going to come out on top.

Initially, I went to the Chapel/Church to hang out for a couple of hours, see people, make a few deals, and see what the other players were up and in to. One day I was sitting in the Chapel as one of my "friends" was singing the "Blood of Jesus." It stirred an emotion within me that I knew was long sense dead. I had been raised in a sanctified home where we went to Church every day, or so it seems. A lot of seeds had been deposited in me. The planting had now met the right climate for germination to take place.

A quaking was taking place in the prison. The Holy Ghost had entered and began to move through some people here. We were in the midst of a Holy Ghost Revival. People from numerous churches were coming inside the prison. Men from every walk of life; the gutter-most to the uttermost. The Holy Ghost was infecting and affecting everybody and anybody. 1997 was a fulfilling year at the prison. The night I got baptized, thirteen others rose out of their seats to be baptized in Jesus' Name. This was the beginning of a long and arduous journey for me. The enemy had seen one of his champions about to go down. The thing about some fights is quite uncanny. You know your opponent, their moves and how they're coming. You plan on it to turn before you are hit with it, and yet in slow motion you are still powerless. We of ourselves can do nothing.

One night the Lord came to me with a clear mandate. LAST CALL! I heeded this urging and declared on December 18th 2004 that I was getting all the junk out of my trunk and let go of all the devil's mess. I found that by emptying the vessel of all unrighteousness, I had become receptive to the things the Lord wanted me plugged into. I began to develop a Bible Study period and timely prayer sessions. On April 4, 2005 I was filled with the Holy Ghost in the recreation yard. Every fiber in me was refurbished. Renewal is an ongoing transition; it's not a wax on wax off. The Holy Ghost is real and frees you from all unrighteousness. The Holy Ghost gave me what I have wanted all my life; to be free. He prepared me for some difficult times.

In an effort to condense forty-two and a-half years behind bars, I must say that people who worked tirelessly in my spiritual growth saw the object of their efforts come to an expected end. With her assignment at an end, my fiancé rested from all her labors. After her, my mama went on to be with the Lord. My niece, uncle, and aunt soon followed. All of them went on to be with the Lord with a unique version, yet a testimony that they had pleased God and lay down with the faith that soon they would arise from The Rest with a Glorified body to Reign with Jesus. The Lord has been good to me. The storms do keep on raging. The temptations do come.

This past season I have been blessed beyond measure to be one of the guitar players for the Christian services. The assignment was not a journey without contention and trepidation. God never said it would be easy. I was given a message last month entitled "What Shall We Do with Jesus?" The Lord really opened my eyes concerning His manifestations. He can take anything He wants and make it into whatever He wants. All He wants is a willing vessel, pliable and heat resistant. We must bear our burden, deny ourselves, and look to Jesus our Redeemer. He brought us back from the fowler to be restored into the family we had become outcast to because of preceding fallen man. If we are in the Father's Will, we shall receive everything He left for us. The Comforter was sent to do just that. Revitalize us until He returns to usher in The Kingdom on high. No man can come to the Father except by Jesus. I thank and Praise the Lord for freeing my soul and for not letting the snare of the fowler triumph over me.

— L.E.

Judgement Day

The Bible promises us a final judgement:

And I saw a great white throne and the one who sat upon it, from whose face the earth and sky fled away, but they found no place to hide. I saw the dead, great and small, standing before God; and The Books were opened, including the Book of Life. And the dead were judged according to the things written in The Books, each according to the deeds he had done. The oceans surrendered the bodies buried in them; and the earth and the underworld gave up the dead in them. Each was judged according to his deeds. And Death and Hell were thrown into the Lake of Fire. This is the Second Death—the Lake of Fire. And if anyone's name was not found recorded in the Book of Life, he was thrown into the Lake of Fire.

Revelation 20:11-5

At the judgement, books are opened. The Books contain every good or bad deed of every person. The book of Life contains the names of those who have put their trust in Christ to save them.

When God judges you, will you be found guilty or innocent? Will you spend eternity (forever) in Heaven or Hell?

To read more "Real Life Stories," go to the next page. For the next truth; skip to page 89.

CHAPTER 16
"No Man Cometh Unto The Father, But By Me"

When I speak of my supernatural search, I speak only of the search through the truth of Jesus Christ by the awesome power of Holy Spirit. (KJV John 14:6 Jesus saith unto him, I am the way, the truth, and the life: no man cometh unto the Father, but by me.)

Many try to seek the supernatural through other means in which they find themselves bound by various spirits of err and opening doors leading them directly to the hand of the enemy. The only true way to seek the supernatural is through Jesus by the direction of the Holy Spirit. He will show you truths only within the boundaries of what you are able to safely understand at any given point in your walk with Jesus. The search for the supernatural is meant to be an incredible journey by which the Father loves to show his children what our hearts desire.

The very beginning of the supernatural didn't begin by my own means of searching God out. It began with God revealing Himself in a very powerful way to me.

I was 17 years old at the time. My 18th birthday was only three weeks away. At this point in my life, I was doing any drug I could get my hands on. I began to sell drugs to support my habit. I had no idea God existed nor did I care. However, even though I was unaware, God began to turn my world upside down only to catch me and reveal His love for me. It all started by a simple thought being placed in my head that unmarked police cars were following me for some reason. With this thought, I began to carefully watch my rearview mirror. My mind began to race as paranoia set in. This paranoia continued over a two week period in which I had stopped use of all and any drugs. I made sure no trace of drugs were in my car. As I drove or walked anywhere, I felt as if anyone could be an undercover officer. I was suspicious of anyone asking a question or even looking at me. It seemed that my whole world was turned upside down, and I had no way of making all this just stop.

I found myself at home most of the time. My mother took notice of this, along with my behavior and began asking me if I was okay. I felt at this point that I had no other place to turn, so I told her everything that had happened over the last two weeks. She really didn't know what to think of my story and most likely thought I was losing my mind. She did the only thing she could think of at the time. She asked if I would come to church with her. This was the last thing I wanted to do. However, I began to think to myself that if the police would see me going to church it would throw them off. With this on my mind, I agreed and off we went.

As I sat in church it seemed like it was crazy hour. Sure they acted nice, but that must be an act. Surely nobody actually believed that they could speak to a man named Jesus that they claimed was God. I left there and never wanted to go back. These people were more crazy then me! Did my own mother get suckered into this as well? As much as I didn't ever want to go back, I did notice that the cars following me began declining as I drove to work and back. Granted I still felt followed, but at least fewer cars were pursuing me. Maybe my little trick worked I thought. My mother again comes to me later in the week asking if I would go to church. I agreed, maybe this time those cops would stop all together.

As the service started, something new happened. It seemed as if the preacher was speaking directly to me this time. In fact, at some point he was so dead on that I began to wonder if my mother had spoke to him before we arrived. Then without any warning I broke down into tears, which turned into complete sobbing as my body trembled from the emotions overtaking me. Just then the preacher asked if any would like to come up and receive Christ Jesus as their Lord and Savior. I found myself standing up without any feeling of weight. It was as if angels were helping me stand to my feet and walk to the front. As I stood up front, I put my hands up in the air, still sobbing as tears ran down my face. I repeated the words the preacher spoke, asking Jesus to save me. After doing this, my crying stopped. I was taken to the backroom, where I was welcomed to the church family and given some material to take home.

So was I now a true believer? Not even close. By the time I got in the car with my mother, I was convinced I had somehow been tricked. However, I couldn't explain the emotions that overtook me. A part of me actually wanted to believe it. I wanted it all to be true, but could it?

On my 18th birthday, my mother asked if I wanted to go to a special Friday night service at the church. She said when got home, we would celebrate my birthday. I agreed to go ahead and go.

This time, I listened closely to the entire service. I also closely watched others. searching for clues as to if all this were real. I wanted to know that my life was more than just random chance and chaos. Towards the end of the service, the speaker began to give a select few people a word that was supposed to come from God. I didn't really believe that God was speaking to this man. But then he did something un-usual. He had everyone bow there heads and close there eyes. Then he said, "There is someone here that Jesus wants to reveal Himself to. Someone who has already confessed Jesus as Lord but still doesn't really believe in this love. Would that person, with all eyes closed, please raise their hand."

I couldn't believe what I had heard. I knew he was speaking of me. I raised my hand slightly, not to be seen. On cue, he continued, "Lord Jesus, you see your child. Show him you are real and love him more than he can even understand." At that moment, something happened to me that is still hard to explain to this day. It can only be compared to an electrical-like surge radiating throughout my entire body. It was like life itself had consumed every part of me. Along with this power-ful feeling going through me, I had such a clear understanding of the immeasurable love Jesus had for me. At that moment, I found that truth was something unlearned but only revealed. No longer could there be any doubt in God's existence. Not only did He exist, He also cared for mankind more than anyone could understand. He was more than just good. He was love in the most perfect and complete way.

It had occurred to me later on that the last three prior weeks were completely orchestrated in order for Jesus to reveal Himself to me. This event has forever changed my view on life and has continued to impact my walk with Jesus even to this day.

— *M.R.T.*

CHAPTER 17
He Has A Plan For Me

Friends, I want to share something with you. This stay here has made me grow strong in my faith. It has gotten me so close with my Lord and Savior Jesus Christ. I know my change is not going to happen overnight. It is a process, a process that started here in prison.

I've come to realize God does things for a reason. He has a plan for each and every one of us. I know He has a plan for me. I started going to the streets at the age of 12, joined a gang at 13, and from there it has been nothing but the wrong ride. I've done all the drugs there are to do and been with many women in the wrong way. I first went to jail at the age of 18 and have been in and out of jail ever since.

I have four lovely children that I love a lot, but I feel I haven't been the father they deserve. My oldest is going to be 14, and I've missed so many years of her life. I couldn't see the problem I had. Both my parents tried to show me the right way. My daughters kept asking why their dad was not in their life – doesn't he love us? I was too busy being involved with drugs, alcohol, women, or in jail.

I got involved with heroin. I had two overdoses with heroin and one with cocaine. I still did what I was doing – my evil ways. I lost both of my two families due to my stays in jail and my drug use.

In 2005, I moved to Texas to try and change my life. I met a girl, and we got together. We had two beautiful children, but my evil was following me. I had a good job in the oilfield until I started messing with crack cocaine. I forgot about my beautiful family and was all about my drinking and drug use. I lost this family too, and I ended up here in prison.

It was here and this time being locked up, that I said to myself, "Enough is enough!" I realized I had to do something different. I needed to break this cycle. I asked God for help, and He answered me. He answered me by making me realize He has been there all along, knocking. I just needed to open the door. He was there to bring me back from the heroin overdoses. I should have been dead. He was there when I got shot and when I walked away from three wrecks that I went through without a scratch. He's always been there looking out for me.

Now, my Lord has helped me open my eyes and look at life in a totally different way. I've come to humble myself, to use this stay here to become stronger in faith, and to become the better person I need to be – first for myself, then for my lovely children. I'm ready to bury my past and join the good ride.

— *Jorge*

CHAPTER 18
God Was There

When your dad wasn't there to love you like he should,
I was there.
When your friends told you that they didn't want to play with you,
I was there.
When people took advantage of you and you didn't know where to turn,
I was there.
When you were at school being bullied around,
I was there.
When the girls you liked turned you down,
I was there.
When you thought that one beer would make you feel better,
I was there.
When you went after women to fill the void in your life,
I was there.
When you spent all your money on the things that you thought
would make you happy, I was there.
When you were in the county jail and thought you were alone,
I was there.

It took going to prison to realize that all the things that I thought would make me happy ended up making things worse. But through all of that, like the prodigal son, God was there with open arms waiting for me to come back to Him. I forgave those who hurt me. I have a closer relationship with my dad. I've talkd more with my dad now that I have before. I've thanked God for my Christian brothers who helped me in my Christian walk. I've drawn closer to God. I now depend on Him for my every need.

— *Garabet*

Note: Garabet was recently released from prison. He is living in a residential Christian re-entry house

Standing on the Fence

I was standing on a fence, and there was an incredibly large group of people assembled around it.

On one side of the group stood a man, Jesus. On the other side of the group stood another man, Satan. Separating them, running through the group, was the fence I was standing on.

Both Jesus and Satan began calling to the people in the group and, one by one, each having made up his or her mind, each went to either Jesus or Satan.

This kept going on, and eventually Jesus had gathered around him a group of people from the larger crowds, as did Satan. But I joined neither group. I stood on the fence. Then Jesus and his people left and disappeared. So too did Satan and his people.

And I was left alone, standing on the fence.

As I stood there, Satan came back. He appeared to be looking for something that he'd lost. I said, "Have you lost something?"

Satan looked straight at me and replied, "No, there you are. Come with me."

"But," I said, "I stood on the fence. I chose neither you nor Him."

"That's okay," said Satan. "I own the fence. You belong to me."

You may go to the next page for more "Real Life Stories," or skip to page 101 for more truth.

CHAPTER 19
Forgiven And Filled

I never dreamed my life testimony at age 58 would be written from prison. I really should not be surprised since I had been running from God and living against Him for 20 years. In fact, I had not truly served Him for 40 years. When asked, I told others I was "a Christian," but who did I think I was kidding? I only deceived myself, not God, and I reaped what I sowed (Gal. 6:7-8).

I can only blame myself. I alone accept full responsibility for my actions. I definitely do not blame God. He didn't cause this. He didn't leave me or forsake me – I was the one who left Him. Neither can I blame my "environment" or my family. I was raised in a middle-class home in a good neighborhood by both parents who were dedicated Christians. I cannot blame the justice system. As a first-time offender, I would never have even been locked up for the past three years if I had only initially obeyed the terms of my probated sentence. It was my own fault. I gave myself over to worldly temptations, pursuits and pleasures. My addictions to drugs, alcohol, sex, and pornography only made matters much worse.

Where did I first "go wrong?" Twenty years ago, my own pride, selfishness, impatience, greed, and lack of self-control devastated a marvelously successful life. At age 37, I was at the top of my profession as a CPA earning a salary well into the six-figures. I had been blessed with a wonderful, Godly wife and a healthy infant son. I had a new custom built home and two nice vehicles. My credit record was spotless. I had credit cards with over $100,000 available credit and, except for my mortgage, was totally free of consumer debt. By any worldly standard, I was "on top of the world."

Outwardly, I was the definition of success. Inwardly I was lost, confused, bored, empty, and restless (Eccl 2:10-11). I realize now I had everything but the one thing that mattered. I did not have God. I was not thankful. I did not desire or seek God. I thought I was wise, but I was a fool (Rom. 1:21-22). My ego, conceit, selfishness, and pride were about to destroy my life (Prov. 16:18).

In 1989, I selfishly left my wife and son to pursue fame and riches in Nashville's music business. I became my own "god," determined to create and control my own life. For this vanity and foolish pride, God gave me over to my own desires, lusts, and addictions. It was a gradual but steady descent over 20 years into sinfulness, depravity, and reprobation (Rom 1:24-32).

Most of the next 20 years were spent as a mental, emotional, and financial wreck. I filed bankruptcy twice. I was severely and constantly in deep depression. From 2002-2008, I was unemployed and existed only by the kindness of strangers and one friend, who loved me in spite of myself. He allowed me to stay free with him for three years. Eventually, I alienated him too. I got an apartment and a menial job for a few months (after I could no longer stay with him) but was soon fired and homeless. It was 2006. I lived in a tent on a wooded hillside in South Nashville for 1 ½ years. Then I lived for 6 months at the a rescue mission. I was there when I was arrested in May, 2008 for violating the terms of my probation. My probated sentence was revoked, and I was sent to a medium security facility to serve my sentence.

I was so empty inside for so many years. In spite of everything I tried, nothing filled the void in my soul. I felt unworthy of love. Over time, I pushed away every friend and family member I had. I was without hope and without God in my world (Eph. 2:12). So often, I wanted to die. I tried several times to take my life, but a merciful and loving God rescued me in spite of myself. Thank God, He was not finished with me yet.

I see now that He had His own plan for my life. He would not begin to reveal it until I finally realized and admitted what a mess and failure I had made after I made myself "god" of my life. My first act of submission was to ask for a Bible from the Chaplain – a Gideon New Testament, which I read daily for about 15 minutes. Ten months later, I "came to myself" like the Prodigal Son (Luke 15:17-18). I had finally reached bottom. I could not go any lower. When I finally surrendered to Him and cried out in true humility and brokenness, God heard me. He lifted me out of the miry pit of hopelessness and despair. He placed my feet solidly on His Rock - Jesus (Psalm 40:1-3).

I realized I could not fully accept God's forgiveness for my many sins without forgiving myself and others. I also knew I had to seek forgiveness from those affected by my pride, selfishness, and other sins. I confessed, sincerely repented, and asked Jesus to take over my life. What a heavy burden of guilt, shame, remorse, and embarrassment I had been carrying. As I sought and gave forgiveness for myself and others, these burdens were lifted off my soul and spirit. Now, instead of those oppressive emotional and spiritual burdens, the Holy Spirit within me has filled me with the incredible lightness of His fruit – more love, real joy, true peace, increased patience, and self-control, etc. (Gal 5:22-24).

On April 20, 2009, my 57th birthday, I re-dedicated my life to Jesus Christ. I have since been re-baptized too. Even though I am still locked up, I am free on the inside! Jesus is not only my Saviour, but He is now truly my Lord and in-charge of all my life. I am determined that my remaining 15-20 years on earth will be drastically different from my most recent 20 years. I am so thankful God impressed upon me to use these last 20 months of confinement as a time to grow spiritually in His Word and be "transformed by the renewing of my mind" (Rom. 12:1-2). God has allowed me to spend this time in spiritual education and Christian life training programs sponsored by the Chaplain. Bible correspondence courses, Chapel service attendance, and personal Bible Study have prepared a solid foundation for me.

I am now a living witness of God's grace, mercy, forgiveness, and power. God has never been more real to me. The differences in me are real and permanent. God has changed me from the inside out. My attitudes, thoughts, desires, and speech have all drastically changed. I am truly a "new creature in Christ – old things are passed away, everything has been made new" (II Cor. 5:17). After having now experienced the fullness, love, joy, and peace of God in Christ Jesus, it is absolutely unthinkable that I would ever again be lured by Satan back into the emptiness, self-hate, anxiety, and depression of that "old man" and his addictions. Truly, God's love and abiding presence of His Holy Spirit have worked a life-saving miracle in me through Jesus Christ!

Now, God has called me to minister to His lost and forgotten children – inmates, ex-cons, homeless, depressed, addicts, and sex offenders. Since I am have recently been "classified" as each one of these, perhaps God will use my experiences to reach others like me for the Kingdom. As I answer God's call on my life to be an ordained and licensed servant of the Lord, I pray God will work through me to bring the hope, love, and grace of Jesus to many who are unloved, lost, hurting, forgotten, needy, despised, depressed, and forsaken – people who are even now just like I once was.

I am humbly and eternally grateful to our God for second chances! My feelings are like those of Paul when he wrote to Timothy nearly 2,000 years ago:

"I thank Christ Jesus our Lord, who has given me strength, that He considered me faithful, appointing me to His service. I was once a blasphemer, a persecutor, and a violent man. I was shown mercy because I acted in ignorance and unbelief. The grace of our Lord was poured out on me abundantly, along with the faith and love that are in Christ Jesus.

Here is a trustworthy saying that deserves full acceptance: Christ Jesus came into the world to save sinners – of whom I am the worst. But for that very reason I was shown mercy so that in me, the worst of sinners, Christ Jesus might display His unlimited patience as an example for those who would believe on Him and receive eternal life. Now to the King eternal, immortal, invisible, the only God, be honor and glory for ever and ever. Amen."

(I Timothy 1:12-17, NIV)

I am and will remain a humble and grateful servant and follower of the Lord Jesus Christ!

—Stephen

On December 29, 2010, I was released from prison. I am living in Texas, where I am being mentored in the Lord and in the prison ministry. On February 23, 2012, I was ordained into the ministry and licensed to preach the gospel of Jesus Christ.

CHAPTER 20
My Brother Sent Someone to The Rescue

On the outside I knew that there was a God. I knew someone had to create all of us. What I didn't know was that Jesus Christ our Savior gave his life for all of our sins. I owned my own company. My wife, myself, and one driver operated our three semi dump trucks. We hauled slag out of the steel mills in Indiana. I drove five days a week, and I worked on the trucks and trailers seven days a week. Any spare time I had was spent with my wife and two children. My son races motocross, so I also had to keep his bike up and running. My daughter was into singing, and pool parties, and wanting to do stuff like going to the movies, shopping, bowling, and mini-golf.

Everything I did was for my family. I neglected spending time with my brother, dad, and sisters. I didn't have time (I thought) to get to know God. I do not want to get into detail as to the exact circumstances of my crime, but I will say that two people lost their lives. I honestly feel that if God was not by my side that day, I would have lost my life. God gave me an inner strength to fight for my life, and I give him all the credit for me being alive. That was my life on the outside.

When I was in the a county jail, a pastor from a church my brother attended took time out of his life to come and visit me to tell me about God and our Savior Jesus Christ. He came to visit me almost every week during my 18 month stay in the county jail. The pastor changed my life and helped me find my Salvation in Jesus Christ. I lost my entire life. My wife was my one and only love, and I lost her forever. My two children do not visit or write to me. I believe that they hate me for what happened that day. I lost my home, business, freedom, and my honest character that I was so proud of on the street. My children lost their mother, father, home, and family security that I worked so hard to provide for them. The other victim's children lost their father. I know if God would not have given me the strength to defend myself that day, I would be the one dead now.

The children lost the most, but if it was not for all of this happening I do not know if I ever would have found God and my Savior Jesus Christ. I have a lot of difficulty at times forgiving myself. At times I get angry about why this all happened and feel like taking my own life. If I didn't have God in my life, I would not have anyone to turn to when time gets rough for me. My life is forever changed thanks to God, Amen.

—C.L.

CHAPTER 21
Mom Called Me
A Loser

Mom called me a "loser."

My Step-Dad told me I was the "stupidest person God ever put breath in!"

I was in California, and it was near the holidays. I went to a pay phone and called home. "You may think you are coming home for Thanksgiving, and you may actually make it to the neighborhood, but don't even think about coming to eat with us – you are a loser and I don't know who you are. You are not the son I gave birth to!" These words came from my mom when I told her I was coming home for the holidays. As I stood at the phone booth, I couldn't believe that my mom had turned on me. Your mom is always supposed to love you no matter what. She explained how I broke her heart over and over. Each time, I made a promise to stop doing drugs, only to break that promise before the week was up. I just stood quietly, holding the phone in disbelief. Then she said the words that finally broke down my wall of denial. "You have ruined all of my holidays for so long. I can't remember when there wasn't a crisis or a call to be bailed out of jail. So when we are at the Thanksgiving table ready to say the prayer . . . while others are saying whatever they are saying to God, I'm going to thank God you are not here!"

For years I had run away, stole the car, set the school on fire, beat people up on the school bus, passed out in the yard, shot drugs, was kicked out of school, sold hot pistols, was kicked out of working for the carnival, jailed several times, divorced, and finally sent to prison;. I believed everyone else was the problem, not me.

When I came back to my old neighborhood, some of my friends from high school had become "Jesus freaks." They invited me to a home Bible study. Naturally, I went because there were pretty women there. I wasn't their dating type, but I continued to go because they treated me with respect, even when I went high and somewhat embarrassing. They tried, but no Jesus freak stuff for me.

Then one of the ladies from the Bible study introduced me to this hillbilly pastor from Missouri. He had come up to be the pastor of an inner city church. I went on Sunday mornings a few times, but the music sounded like funeral music to me. I just could not get into the hymns. I went to one Sunday night service and realized it was one of the services where they tried to get all the "sinners to come to the altar." My pride was not going to let that happen.

The pastor made a call on me one day when I was in my garage drinking and smoking joints with my friends. The door was open, so he just came in and sat down with us. He started talking about regular, everyday things. We tried to hide the pot and beer, but we all knew he saw it. He said nothing about it. Then he looked at me and said, "I'd like you and your friends to come to the service this Wednesday." I told him it was my birthday and Halloween, so I probably wouldn't be able to come. He jokingly said, "If you and all your friends come Wednesday night, I'll sing happy birthday to you."

I went that Halloween night to the Wednesday service. It was strange. This service was different than the Sunday morning gig or the "drag the sinners to the altar" service on Sunday nights. People just sang a song, then someone would stand and talk about how God had helped them that week. Someone else might read a special verse that meant something to them, and then they would break out in song again. I just couldn't figure out how each person knew when it was their time to stand or say something. I had worked at the carnival and there was always some kind of gimmick; especially at the machine gun stand where you try and shoot out the red star – my old job.

At the close of the service he "opened the altar" for anyone who wanted to pray. I really didn't understand the church language but my heart was pounding hard. I fought it and remained in my seat. After the service, I met the pastor at the door. Once again he was kind, but it was as if he could see right though me. "Do you have any questions about tonight?" I said I had a few. He offered to meet with me in his office. I ended up kneeling down at a metal folded chair repeating a prayer he said. I told him I did not know how to pray. He told me, "Just say the words I say, but if you don't mean them don't say them. God will do the work in your heart if you are honest." I wish I could remember what the words of the prayer were. I do not. When I got up from kneeling I said, "Is that all there is to it?" He said, "As long as you were honest with God and repented of those sins then you are a New Creature in Christ." "Are you sure?" I asked. I did not cry. I did not sniffle. I really didn't feel any emotions. So I left and went on my way.

Later that night as I lay awake in bed thinking about what I'd done that night, my memory was flooded with all the bad things I'd done in my life. I thought about all the people I'd hurt and sold drugs to. I thought about the friend who died of an overdose, who never used drugs until I introduced him to them. Each time a thought would come up, a wave of guilt would come over me. I didn't see anything, no vision or anything like that, but it was like my sins came up written on the sand of the beach and then a wave would come and wash away what had been written. I started to cry and could not stop. For the first time in my life, I felt clean.

I started going to Sunday services and the music still sounded like funeral music to me, but that didn't matter. I even went to Sunday School and started to learn how to find the different books of the Bible. It blew me away when I heard the story of Jonah and the big fish! I'd never heard that one before. I just plain craved reading the Bible. For the first three weeks someone at the church called me or invited me to something at the church. I wasn't working, so my schedule was always open. Then it hit me one Sunday morning. "I haven't drank or done any drugs in weeks!" I went to the pastor and asked him what did you do to me so I don't want to do drugs?" Naturally, he told me,

"It wasn't me. It was the Lord who took the desire away." The loser had been loosed by the power of God.

That was over three decades ago. Since that time, I can't even describe all He has done for me. He repaired many of the relationships I destroyed. He made the way for me to enter college and even go on for graduate school, all of it paid for. He made the way each time I enrolled in another semester. Now I own my own business. I'm married again. My children have never seen me use drugs, drink, or do any of the other foolishness of the past. Old things have truly become obsolete in my life. I really am that "New Creature" the pastor told me I'd become on Halloween night. On my birthday, I can celebrate my natural birth and my spiritual birth at the same time. The most unusual thing happened along the way. The very place I said I'd never come back to if God ever let me out of prison; well, that is the place he called me to go and minister. My misery became my ministry.

"For I know the plans I have for you," declares the LORD, "plans to prosper you and not to harm you, plans to give you hope and a future. Then you will call on me and come and pray to me, and I will listen to you. You will seek me and find me when you seek me with all your heart." Jeremiah 29:11-13 NIV

— *Aharon*

Day Of Redemption

Jesus gave His Blood, His Life, so all your sins could be forgiven. Jesus paid your penalty for sin; in full.

Now it's up to you to accept or reject what Jesus has done for you.

If you repent for breaking God's Law and put your trust in Jesus, when God looks at you, He will not see a liar, a thief, an adulterer, or a law breaker but he will see a person that Jesus has redeemed from the curse of the Law, one that Jesus paid the full penalty for their sin. God will see the Blood of Jesus that has washed you as white as snow. Only through Jesus can you be right with God.

You may go to the next page for more "Real Life Stories," or skip to page 118 for more truth.

CHAPTER 22
The Gardener's Hand

I was born in Germany in 1955 to middle-class parents and a father who was a lifer in the U.S. Navy. Our family moved to a different military base every two or three years. Often the moves were from one country to another. The frequent moves, steady loss of friends, and changes in culture were difficult. It was also difficult growing up with ADHD and with a father who often took his frustration out through emotional and physical abuse. Nevertheless, I learned to cover well, hiding behind an empty smile.

My mother and father divorced when I was eleven. I was relieved when he was no longer in my life. At the time, I didn't realize how angry I was inside. In addition to my father's abuse, I was homosexually abused when I was 4 years old. It was as if a pencil-sized hole had been poked through my soul as a child. As I grew, the hole grew as well.

Throughout my teen years, I rebelled. My first drink was at age twelve. I got drunk, got sick, and passed out. By the time I was thirteen, I was huffing glue, gasoline, and spot remover. I started smoking marijuana and hash at age fourteen, taking hallucinogens and speed at age fifteen, using barbiturates and Quaaludes at age sixteen, and shooting Demerol, Morphine, and whatever at age seventeen. I was an alcoholic and drug addict. I sold drugs to keep myself in supply.

Alcohol and drugs created chaos, heartache, and confusion. I experienced blackouts, lost time, losing my left leg in an accident, arrests, and finally overdose on Demerol when I was nineteen years old. In an attempt to change, I laid down the syringe, pills, and pot. I picked up the bottle, thinking I would do better. Alcohol became my drug of choice.

I got married and got a good job within a year. Shortly thereafter, I fathered two beautiful daughters. After three arrests for alcohol related offenses, I was arrested in 1982 for public intoxication and criminal recklessness with a weapon. Extremely intoxicated on alcohol and hash, I drove to the police station. I left my car in the middle of the road and walked into the station wielding a loaded shotgun. I was thinking I would get help to find my wife, who I believed had been kidnapped. My wife was hiding in the neighbor's apartment because she was afraid of me. The court gave me two option: prison or treatment. I chose treatment. It's during treatment that I recalled being sexually abused as a young boy. I wanted to change but did not know how to fix myself. While I believed in a god, I did not understand my God. And for good reason, he was not the God of the Bible and was no god at all. As a result, I had no spiritual conversion and just remained dry (not sober) and drug free (not clean) for the next twelve years. Still, I was self-absorbed, deeply troubled, and emotionally immature.

During this time, my wife and I divorced. I was a single adult with a good job and an emptiness that I could not fill. I was no longer using drugs and alcohol, and I turned to sex to try to fill the emptiness. That didn't fill the emptiness inside. I tried college part-time and working full-time, graduating with a 3.96 GPA and a double major in business administration and addiction counseling. That didn't fill the emptiness inside either. I served on two community boards along with the mayor, police chief, fire chief, doctors, psychologists, teachers, and representatives from all sectors of the community. That still didn't fill the emptiness inside.

In my mid-thirties, I decided to settle down and get married again. I married a beautiful woman with a good career. That didn't fill the emptiness inside. I started working more hours; fifty, sixty, seventy hours per week. I was thinking if I just had more money, I would be happy. That didn't fill the emptiness inside. I desperately tried to fill the hole with anything I could find. No matter what I tried, I couldn't escape the ache of anguish and the echo of emptiness in my soul. Desperate and out of options, I consulted a psychologist and psychiatrist who diagnosed me with ADHD and depression. He prescribed Prozac for the depression and Ritalin and Dexedrine, for the ADHD.

I filled the prescriptions. After thirty days of taking the medicine as prescribed, I found myself in a pharmacy buying syringes, taking the pills home, crushing them up, and injecting Ritalin and Dexedrine. I did it over and over, every day, all day. I hadn't used a syringe in twenty years. I thought that part of my life was behind me.

In the thirteen months that I was strung out on speed, my life spiraled out of control. While extremely intoxicated on alcohol and Klonipin, I shot four innocent men after a traffic accident, killing three and rendering paralyzed the fourth shooting victim. I was convicted of three counts of murder and one count of attempted murder. I was sentenced to life without parole plus one hundred eighty years in March 1997.

Without hope, and now in prison, a two-time convict took me under his wing and taught me how to make wine. Soon, I was getting drunk, smoking marijuana, and shooting heroin and cocaine. I was right back in the same pathetic mess that landed me in prison.

During this time, I was working in prison industries next to a convict who was a born-again Christian. He never missed an opportunity to talk to me about his friend, Jesus. I didn't want to hear it, but I was working along-side of him and couldn't get away. To make things worse, it seemed as though he would wait to talk to me until I was hung-over or crashing from a two or three day binge. It got to the point where I would do a 180 and go hide from him as soon as I saw him coming. One day, I found myself hiding in the toilet stall. I was peering through the crack in the door, waiting until the coast was clear.

He was a very patient and determined man. He shared his personal testimony and reminded me that I didn't have to live this way any longer, that there was a different way in Jesus. I can't tell you exactly when I stopped running from him and started running to him, but I did after I realized that he had something that I didn't have. He had peace and joy that certainly didn't come from behind these walls. This went on for several months. One day, I came to the end of myself. Tired, desperate, and hopeless, I came to work to find him waiting on me. He asked simply, "You're ready, aren't you?" All I could do is cry.

He invited my to meet him in the recreation yard later, where I received the gift of eternal life through the blood of Jesus. Hallelujah! Immediately, the desire to drink and do drug was gone. A peace came over me that I'd never felt before. God did for me what I was unable to do for myself. For twenty years, I had tried to fix myself but utterly failed. For the first time in my life, I knew I was going to be okay, even though I didn't know how.

My eyes were opened, and I soon came to realize that when I received Jesus as my Lord and Savior, He filled the emptiness that nothing else could fill. Praise the Lord! I surrendered my life to the Lord on January 9, 1998.

As a part of God's plan, my mother and father reunited in marriage after thirty years of divorce. They came to know Jesus as their Lord and Savior. Since my rebirth in Jesus, the Lord has healed me and restored my relationship with my father. Now, it is my privilege and delight to fellowship with him in the Lord. I receive his godly counsel and feel the love of a father that I never knew could be so fulfilling.

The Lord gave me wisdom and the opportunity to share my friend

Jesus with my two daughters, in the prison visiting room. Prayerfully patient and determined over the years, I shared my testimony and the Word of God. The Lord was faithful in answering my prayers. First, my youngest daughter, who was following in my footsteps, surrendered her life and received Jesus as Lord. Then, my oldest daughter, after eight years of persistent prayer, surrendered her heart to Jesus while visiting me in prison. The Lord gave me the honor and privilege of leading her in a prayer and confession of faith unto eternal life. What a blessing!

It's humbling to think how Jesus has prepared me, over the years, for the work that He has called me to do behind these walls. He helped me settle in my spirit that there are much worse fates than spending the rest of my life in prison. I'm grateful because that can be such a distraction. Jesus has given me the grace to have had faithful men disciple me. They took the time to teach, counsel, and love me. As a result, His Holy Spirit has rooted me in His Word, brought me into the knowledge of Jesus and His truth, raised me up, regenerate my soul, restored my family and much of what the devil had stolen, set me on a new course with a new purpose, and empowered me to be a witness of the gospel of Jesus Christ. He has given me the opportunity and the presence of mind to give, as I have been given to advocate for those who have no voice, to have a heart for those less fortunate, and to have the patience and wisdom necessary to love others, because He first loved me.

God forgave all of my sins, and He gave me a heart to never forget. I am reminded daily that my selfish choices robbed children of their fathers, fathers of their sons, grandchildren of their grandpa, families of their innocence and security, and created unimaginable pain and suffering for the surviving victim and his family. Everyday the stain of innocent blood on my hands reminds me of the empty chair at the tables of the victims' families. Their pain brings me sadness. Their loss brings me sorrow. This is my deepest regret and my greatest anguish. I am so sorry for what I did. I wish I could take it back…So, I pray and trust God to do what only He can do—heal the broken hearted and save the lost; for I know that it is only by His grace that I live..

My prayer is that you will draw near to God in humble adoration, laying aside every distraction, and seek His face and pursue Him, that you might know Him.

— *D.T.S.*

CHAPTER 23
My Search
For Love

I was born and raised in Illinois. I'm from a middle class family. My upbringing was less than perfect. There was a lot of fighting and strife in my home. I love my family, and my parents did the best they could, so that's all I'm going to say about that.

As a young girl and into womanhood, I was always looking for love. I wanted that fairy tale white knight that would come rescue me from all that was wrong with the world and save me from myself. This mind-set directly led to the addictions I developed: alcohol, pot, cocaine/crack, prescription drugs, and eventually heroin. My search for love and my need to fill a void led to very unhealthy relationships. When I was 15, I lost my virginity to a 25 year old married man. I was this family's babysitter from the time I was 13. I guess by the time I turned 15, this man thought I was woman enough to do as he pleased. I thought I was mature. I was for my age, but not mature enough for that, emotionally or any in other way. I thought I was in love with him, and he told me he was in love with me. To make a long story short, his wife found out. My whole world was turned upside down. I lost him, her (who was at one time my best friend), and their kids that I had grown to love like they were my own. I was more than just the babysitter. I was their friend. I hung out there every weekend, they were kind of… my life. So it was a pretty devastating time. That whole situation pretty much set the tone for my future relationships with men. From here on, it was a life of bad relationships, drugs, and alcohol. It seemed that with every new man came a new drug and a new demon for me to inherit.

Later that year when I was still 15, I met my first real boyfriend. He was 20 years old. He turned out to be physically abusive and very controlling. During that relationship, I dropped out of high school and had my first child at the age of 18. I ended up leaving him when my son was 5 months old. I got a fake I.D. and starting hitting the bars. It wasn't long before I had a serious drinking problem and started using cocaine due to meeting abuser #2. He was 10 years older than me and was going through a divorce. He supplied me with plenty of cocaine. He was nice and sympathetic to my situation, but he soon turned abusive too. The beatings were far worse than the first boyfriend. The drugs were out of control, and so was the abuse. With him I suffered physical, mental, and emotional abuse and even rape. I had two more children with him. In my mind, there was no way out. So I stayed and suffered for 10 years. During those years he and I both picked up a bad habit with hydrocodone. This was on top of the daily cocaine use. I was arrested for my first felony, picking up a fraudulent prescription in Illinois. While out on bond for that charge, I was arrested in Indiana for the same thing. I was 28.

I was so dependent on the drug that the physical withdrawals made me want to die. When you are in bondage to a drug that you are physically sick without, you'll do whatever you can to ease the pain. At the time I was taking forty 10mg pills a day. That is about 8 times the maximum amount prescribed to take in a day. I lost 50 pounds because it made me so sick I usually threw up about 5 times a day. I am very fortunate to be alive. I finally got away from him because he went to prison. However, I was lost without him. I know that sounds crazy, but when you are controlled by an abuser for so long you end up losing any existence of your own. I was with him from age 19 to age 29, so it was like he practically raised me. It's pretty sick thinking, I know. I was left with three kids. I was evicted, had lost my job, and had no car.

I was on probation for my two felonies. After about two weeks of a horrible detox, I had finally kicked the pills. However, as any addict does, I just traded one addiction for another. I was living from place to place, drinking heavily, and just continued to be lost. I had to eventually give my kids to their father's family. I wasn't fit to take care of them, and I didn't have a stable home for them to live in. I still saw my kids here and there, but eventually my selfishness led me far from them. I was too focused on my path to self-destruction to care about anything else. There were brief spaces of time where I really tried to get my act together and had a game plan to make things better. I even put myself in rehab several times. It never took. I always fell again and always worse than the time before.

Then entered Brad, who is now my husband. I know what your thinking, "Oh, he must be that knight in shining armor she was looking for all her life." That's not even close... Brad and I met in a bar and started seeing each other. Very soon, we fell madly in love. He was different from the others, he never hit me or called me names. He was peaceful and mellow. We had big dreams. We talked about getting married and having a home and babies. The devil had other plans for us first.

Bars were our thing for the most part. He had told me about his addiction to heroin, but he was clean from it at that point, as far as I knew. Before long, his demon became my demon, and we starting using heroin together. Our lives very quickly fell to pieces, not that they were ever really together. We were drenched in sin.

We stole from family and friends. We burned every bridge we had. My family completely let me go and would have nothing to do with me. I was shooting $200 worth of heroin a day. My daily life was a vicious circle of stealing, pawn shops, and getting to the west side of Chicago to get my drug. Every day was a race against the withdrawals, a panic to get my drug before I got sick. Nothing else mattered. We were homeless, hopeless, and soulless. It was a sick existence. We slept in hallways of roach infested slums on the west side. We begged for money on the street and stole from anyone we could.

Heroin is pure concentrated evil. You become a slave to it. Nothing else matters, and it is the closest I will ever come to being demon possessed. I think back to the end of these days and remember how I just wanted to die. I was utterly hopeless and without purpose. I remember shooting up and praying it would be the shot that killed me. I desperately wanted to end my suffering. I wanted to end the monster I was and end the pain I was inflicting on others. I was empty and broken down so deep I couldn't see any glimpse of light.

I ended up violating my probation in both states and went to jail. After another horrible detox and 6 months in county jails, I was sentenced to a work release program. This was the turning point in my life. I have to express the sheer genius of God's perfect plan. The program had just opened up for women. Had it worked out any other way, I would have gone to prison and would not have met the people I did. God worked through every one of them. They were perfectly placed in my life to help me grow into the person I am today.

Now let me tell you about the people God used the most, to show me a way out of the darkness and into His glorious light. While in the program, I met Pastor Michael. He worked there teaching a couple different classes I attended. He is my shepherd and has been there for me through so much. I'm surprised he didn't fire me from the church last year. I was very needy and called him as much as 20 times a day during a time my husband went thru a very hard time. I also met Adele, who was the praise and worship leader at the church. She came into the program and taught bible studies every week. Almost immediately, I felt a pull toward her. I know now that the pull I felt was actually toward Jesus that lives in her. During one of her bible studies, I accepted Jesus into my life. At another bible study after that, I was telling her some of my concerns and I was being released soon. I had nowhere to go, no money, and no one who cared anymore. I didn't even have anyone to pick me up when I got out. Adele said "Well, I'll pick you up. We will find somewhere for you to go, don't worry." To most people this probably seems trivial, but it was this small act of kindness that won my heart to the Lord. In that moment Jesus revealed to me that I was never again going to be alone. Adele saw me through God's eyes. Through my eyes, I saw God in her.

By the time I was released, I had arranged for another ride. After I was picked up, I was literally left out on the street. The person who picked me up lied about the fact that he arranged somewhere for me to stay. Once that fell through, he just left me there. I called Adele. She picked me up, and our church put me up at a motel. Adele took me, got me some food, and provided me with the things I needed. To make a long story short, I ended up going to live in a bad situation. I was reading my bible every day and going to church. I was seeing my kids every day and doing my best to block out the evil around me, but it was starting to slither back into my life. That's what the enemy does. But God!!!! Like God does, He pressed my life once again to repentance. One day after a violent, abusive situation with the person I was living with, God said, "Enough!" I called Adele and cried out to her that I needed help. She and her husband came to pick me up and took me into their home. Keep in mind, I was pretty much a stranger. I was an acquaintance at best. They both knew that I had been a junkie, a thief, and a liar for the greater part of my life. Because God spoke and told them, "Take her, raise her up in Me, and I will do great and mighty things in her," I am here today. All glory to God, but I also have to thank Paul and Adele for their total obedience and for heeding the voice of the Lord rather than listening to their own fears. They've never expressed any fears to me, but I'm positive they must have had them. During my time with them, I was immersed in the word of God and the things of God. It was because God had given me a thirst for Him. It was never forced upon me. We became family. They call me daughter, and I call them mom and dad. They taught me, counseled me, scolded me, corrected me, loved me, and never gave up on me through thick and thin. I know I can be stubborn and rebellious, but God has done a mighty work in me and He is not done yet. Now, it is clear to me that Paul and Adele were pre-destined to be my spiritual parents and me their spiritual daughter.

I started writing to Brad as soon as I moved into Adele's house. He was in prison at the time. I wrote him in one letter "Hey, ya know that thing we have been looking for all our lives? I found it!" I starting telling him about a man named Jesus. He wrote back saying, "You're gonna be a Bible thumper now? Seriously?" Well, Brad ended up getting saved and baptized by the Holy Spirit with evidence of tongues in prison.

Over the last 4 years that I've been saved, God has done miraculous things in my life. First of all, He saved my life and my soul. He has delivered me from drugs, alcohol, and cigarettes. I mean delivered! There is absolutely nothing inside of me that desires any of that anymore. That part of me is dead and gone. Who the Son sets free, is free indeed! He gave me a job and then a better job. All my relationships with my family have been restored. My kids are back with me and am raised up in the Lord. We've gone from a one bedroom three bedroom house and from one vehicle to two. The and strengthened my marriage, after a brief separation when first got home from prison. The devil tried to tear our marriage a but God!!! My life now is to serve the Lord, Adele passed the torch, and I now teach bible studies at the program, where I got saved. I have earned my G.E.D and am now attending college to earn my bachelor's degree in the science of criminal justice with a concentration in human services. My goal is to become a substance abuse counselor. Who better to understand addiction than a former junkie, right? Doors are being opened all the time for me to reach the unreachable. I thank God and just pray He uses me for His glory more and more every day. These are by far the best years of my life, and it's only just begun. I have faith, not to mention proof that God can do exceedingly, abundantly, far beyond all I could imagine. He has made me the head and not the tail. He has set me above and not beneath. His plan for me is for good and not for evil, to give me a hope and a future! It's all for His glory! And the best part of it is, if He will do it for me, He will do it for anyone who calls on his Holy name!

Friend, are you searching for love like I was? Are you looking for love in all the wrong places? Has your search left you addicted to drugs or alcohol? Has your search caused you to do things you never thought you would do? Do you want the white knight that rescued me to rescue you? He will if you ask Him! Call out to Him right now!

— *Laura*

CHAPTER 24

Complete Transformation in Jesus

I was born on a Navy base to an 18 year old mom. My dad was gone much of the time, so my mom raised me by herself. As a child, I was very sickly with bronchitis, asthma, and high fevers. Later, my mom and dad had two more daughters. Because I was the oldest, I suffered the brunt of their abusiveness. I was mistreated physically, emotionally, and mentally. My parents were never shown love by their families, so it stood to reason they didn't know how to show love to their children.

The abuse I suffered took a terrible toll on my life, even at a very young age. At 8 years of age, I began drinking alcohol and taking drugs from a little girl in my neighborhood whose parents were motorcycle "bikers." I stopped coming home, staying with her family whenever possible. I had run away to escape from the abuse, constant restrictions, and punishment for my wayward behavior.

At 12 years old, I was raped. It was so horrible. I associated it with "love" and decided if that's what love was, I wanted no part of it. I was raped frequently through my teen-age years. My heart became very hardened. I built walls of self-protection around my life trying, to keep myself safe.

In junior high school, I partied as hard as I could. I managed to get good grades in spite of it. I had a wonderful first boyfriend, Danny, who had a band. We had so much fun partying and playing all our favorite songs.

I was in the 10th grade, about age 16, when Danny joined the Navy. I was very upset and felt a great sense of loss and rejection when he left. Unknown to Danny, I was pregnant with our baby. I miscarried before I even told him about it. I started selling drugs with a girlfriend, trying to ease the pain of losing Danny and our baby.

At 17, my friend and I were raped by students in our school. Again, I was devastated, scared, and began looking for love anywhere I could find it. In my senior year before graduation, I met and married Willie. I didn't graduate. Willie was an alcoholic, and I was a drug addict. It wasn't exactly a marriage made in heaven! Willie and I had an awesome daughter who we named Brandy. We later divorced during a time I was using crystal meth. This is a very evil drug that seems to take away your pain, but it makes people do evil things. It is definitely from the pit of hell. It causes you to go crazy and eats the calcium right out of your bones.

Against Brandy's advice, I later married a man named Frank. She told me he was evil. I didn't listen to her, and all hell broke loose. It turned out, he was into the occult and in the mafia. We were married for 1½ years during which time he abused Brandy and I sexually, mentally, and physically. When I tried to divorce Frank, he threatened to kill me. I was afraid of what would happen to Brandy if he did kill me, so I gave Brandy to my mother for her protection.

During the years of 1984 through 1989, I lived on the streets in California. I had a brother named Ronnie, who was from my old school. He taught me the biker way of living…with love and respect. We talked about God all the time. In January of 1987, he was shot in his stomach and nearly died. I prayed and begged God to keep him alive. He did! When I told Ronnie how I had prayed, he yelled at me and said, "Why did you do that?" He would have much rather have gone to be with Jesus! I told him that I loved him and would miss him. He told me once that three men wiser than him would come into my life. I was surprised to hear him say that and wondered what it meant. Ronnie was later murdered. Even during the worst of times, I felt protected by angels.

For awhile, I lived on the streets of San Diego. One day, while in a park picking through clothes which had been donated by a church, a woman walked up to me and asked me if I was Denise and said my last name. She recognized me from a picture my mom had of me. She told me mom wanted me back home. I couldn't have been more surprised. It was at this point that things began to change for the better for me. I felt love for the first time in a long time.

However, in September of 1989, I was arrested for being drunk in public. While in jail, a woman began writing letters to me about Jesus. I started getting very curious about this man called Jesus. The guards introduced me to Chaplain Romie who told me the whole story of how Jesus died and rose again. She said that while He was on the cross, I was on His mind and in His heart. She told me that He was in heaven praying for me. I was very overwhelmed by what she said to me. On my way back to my cell, I overheard a Bible study leader saying, "Jesus loves you."

I held back tears, not wanting to let anybody see me cry. I had been in jail for eight days and just had to get out of there. Later, I got down on my knees out in the yard and said, "God, I know You are so real to me. You provided everything I needed when I was on the streets. I can see that now. Your Son, Jesus did this for me, and I will do everything for You. Please deliver me from meth, prison, the streets, sex, and pot. I accept Your Son Jesus in my heart and life forever." I added one more prayer, "Lord, because I was so touched by those letters sent to me in prison, telling me about Jesus, please open Your doors for me to write to your children until Jesus comes for us all."

I suddenly felt a deep and great sense of peace. I felt completely clean and refreshed with an indescribable love. I wept in total gratitude, feeling better than I could ever remember feeling. God came in a very real, tangible way to my heart and mind, soul and spirit. It was the ultimate love I had been searching for from the time I was a very little girl throughout my whole life.

I went back inside to find out I had been called into court and released with a very minimal fine and dropped charges. It was my birthday gift from God, September 13, 1989. I was ecstatic, to say the least!

From jail I went into a women's discipleship home until it closed. I went back to my hometown to help take care of my granddad Dave until 1993. This is when the doors opened for me to step into my Daddy God's ministry, which I named Jesus' Prayer Ministry. We celebrated 19 years of ministry this year. We write letters all over the United States to prisoners, encouraging them in Jesus. God has added to the ministry by sending Worship Leaders, Chaplains, and Teachers. It is awesome to be part of His ministry! I have since discovered who the three wiser men are that Ronnie told me about! They are my blood brother Jesus, my teacher and coach the Holy Spirit, and my precious Father God.

My mother and I have reconciled, and she helps me with the prison ministry. We also enjoy one another's company as friends going to movies, working puzzles, and praying together.

In 2006, I moved back to California wanting to be there on Mother's day to see my mom. I didn't have a ride. I was feeling sad that I couldn't be with her, so I began to worship and praise the Lord. Jesus gave me a vision of my son Vito and my friend Ronnie. They were in heaven with Jesus right next to them. We did a group hug, giving me the best Mother's Day present ever!

God's love is so real in my life, and I pray everyday for more and deeper things from my God. I particularly love 1 John 4:7-19 and ask that you read it as a gift from me to you.

If you have been looking for love in all the wrong places or if you have suffered abuse and hardships, honestly believe that Jesus will come and bring His healing love to your heart. All you have to do is get on your knees and ask Jesus to come into your heart and be Lord and Savior of your life. Ask Him to forgive your sins. He will because He loves you so deeply.

— *Denise*

Day Of Salvation

How do I get saved from the curse of the law? How do I get saved from being forever separated from God? How do I get saved from the Fires of Hell?

1. Admit that you have broken God's Law.
2. Ask God to forgive you.
3. Confess Jesus as the Son of God.
4. Confess that Jesus died on the cross for your sins.
5. Confess that Jesus arose from the dead.

The Bible says:

For salvation that comes from trusting Christ — which is what we preach --- is already within easy reach of each of us; in fact, it is as near as our own hearts and mouths. For if you tell others with your own mouth that Jesus Christ is your Lord, and believe in your own heart that God has raised him from the dead, you will be saved. For it is by believing in his heart that a man becomes right with God; and with his mouth he tells others of his faith, confirming his salvation. For the Scriptures tell us that no one who believes in Christ will ever be disappointed. Jew and Gentile are the same in this respect; they all have the same Lord who generously gives his riches to all those who ask him for them. Anyone who calls upon the name of the Lord will be saved.

Romans 10:8-13

For more "Real Life Stories," turn to next page. To get saved, go to page 129.

CHAPTER 25
I Sold My Brother's Birthday Gift To Buy Myself Ice Cream

I burned down the neighbor's garage.

I skipped school and didn't care about my grades.

I lied about everything.......

I remember it was my brother's birthday, I think I was around 5 years old. I remember selling his birthday gift for enough money to buy an ice cream from the ice cream truck. It seemed like everything went bad from there. I burned down the neighbor's garage. I skipped school, didn't care about my grades, and lied about everything. As I got older I would steal from my parents. I was out of control. I dropped out school at the age of 17. At that time, you could still join the military without a diploma. I managed to make it through 4 years of the navy and couldn't wait to go home to start my life. Boy what a life I started. I started using cocaine at 21 years old and then selling. I was in and out of trouble all the time. I met Dina, my wife to be, at a gas station. We had unprotected sex, and she got pregnant. We married after a few months. I was still using, and we divorced within two years. I remember a man named Clarence. It was Halloween of 1994, and he introduced me to a new way of using cocaine. It was called crack cocaine. By March or April of 1995, I was evicted from my apartment.

I moved to Alabama and away from drugs, so I thought. I got remarried to Rhonda, found crack cocaine again, and was divorce and shipped back to Indiana on a greyhound bus with nothing. My first wife who had rededicated her heart to the Lord was the only one that would take me in. I had burned every bridge I ever crossed. It wasn't the right move for us, so I moved in with my mother. After stealing everything she had, stealing from the pastor of the church, and spending almost 4 years in prison, I found a job as plumber. After 5 years of smoking crack every day, spending every penny of every check every week, drinking, gambling, and being alone, I asked myself what I wanted my life to be. I had stayed in contact with my wife. I told her that I still loved her. I knew it would never work with her serving the Lord and me serving everything else.

God poured His grace on me even when I didn't deserve it. I'm still alive because of it. I finally began to take God serious. I'm like an onion. He's working on me layer after layer. My flesh is weak, but God's grace is never ending. I'm happy to report I have not used drugs, gambled, or drank in almost two years. I'm remarried to my first wife Dina, and I recently got my Journeyman's License for plumbing. I'm going to be fifty this year. Dina and I are going to the jail to help the lost. For people such as ourselves who saw no hope, I hope that they can see what we have and will want the same. I should be dead, but God saw something I didn't. What the devil meant for bad, God turned for good. Doors are being pushed opened. God is healing me. For 26 years I was a drug addict, a liar, and a thief. I know now I'm none of those things. I'm covered by the blood of the lamb. Oh, how I love the Lord!

Friend, do you feel like everything is going bad for you? Have drugs, drinking, gambling, or some other addiction got a hold on you? Do you find yourself lying about everything, like I did? Is your life out of control? Need Help? Want Help? You can find hope just like I did! Call out to Jesus today!

— *Randy*

CHAPTER 26
There Was A Lot Of Disappointment...

It was constant let downs and lies.....

I had a lot of anger, resentment, and hatred........

I was born in Chicago, Illinois in 1982 to a middle class family. I have one sister who is three years older than me. My parents got a divorce when I was about five years old. My dad was an alcoholic but got sober for a part of his life. I believe it was for about thirteen years, but that came to an end. We had to move to a suburb of Chicago because my mom couldn't afford the bills. We moved into a two bedroom condominium in Schaumburg. There was a lot of disappointment from my dad. He would promise to see us and promise to take us for weekends. He did a few times, but it wasn't enough. It was constant let downs and lies. This caused me a lot of anger, resentment, and hatred.

My mom was doing her best with what she had. She worked two to three jobs to provide for my sister and me. This also caused anger in me because she was working and barely home. My sister tried to take on a role of the adult. My thinking was, "You're not my mom, so I don't care what you say." Even when my mom was home, I didn't do what she asked. I was very rebellions, even at a young age.

I began experimenting with weed, cigarettes, and alcohol at age 11. By junior high, I was not only smoking pot but also selling it. I was snorting cocaine and eating acid and mushrooms. In high school I went to get drugs, sell drugs, and find out where the parties were. Somehow I made it to my junior year and got kicked out for fighting with my assistant principal. I was involved in sports but getting high was more important. I ended up getting expelled. Since I had a job, I would just work more. There came a point where a few of my friends had begun using heroin. I knew about it and swore I would never do it, but that soon went out the window. There was a void in my life and in my heart that I was trying to fill. I was trying to take all the pain, anger, and hatred I had in me away. Different drugs worked for awhile and then I had to find something a little stronger. Eventually heroin did just that. Heroin took all my pain and worries away, so I thought. In reality, all the drugs were doing was masking these feelings. Heroin slowly began adding to the anger I was feeling and to the problems I was having in my life.

My job wasn't enough to support my habit, so I began stealing anything I could from anywhere possible. My mom, sister, nephews, aunts and uncles, friends, neighbors, and any retail store felt the wrath of my addiction. It began with snorting the dope, but soon I graduated to shooting it. I was seventeen the first time I tried heroin. This was also the first time I got arrested. I went to county jail, my car got impounded, and it was a rude awakening. I had no drugs because I just did them all. My license and insurance were expired. My mom bailed me out with money my uncle lent her. I swore I was done, but as soon as I got home I was in a hurry to find a friend to go to the west side with. Within an hour, I was on my way.

This life at the time seemed fun. It started out as just getting high but soon became a need and no longer recreation. This went for years. I was a full time employee of Satan himself, and the benefits were horrible. In fact, there was not a single benefit he offered except three hot meals and a cot when I got locked up. By the time I was in my twenties I had been kicked out of my mom's house so many times I can't even count them. I would bounce from friends' houses to motels to cars. Yet I still felt like this was the life I was meant to live. I thought my purpose in life was to be a homeless dope fiend until I overdosed and died or got killed robbing a dope spot on the west side. Eventually, I checked myself into a rehab. For a split second, I thought maybe there is something better for me. As soon as I was out and in a halfway house for a few months, right back to the dope I went. I once again lost all hope. There were quite a few rehabs I checked into, but none of them could help with what I was feeling. Meetings, rehabs, halfway houses; it was just the motions addicts went through. My heart wasn't in it. I wanted out of that lifestyle and vicious cycle, but there was never certainty, assurance, or promise. So my demon kept on keeping on.

I met my wife in a bar when I was 24. At this time I wasn't shooting, but that didn't last long. Soon I was going off with "friends" to get high and lying to her about where I was and what I was doing. Eventually, my demon became hers. We were both off and running to hell in a hand basket. We got married in April 2008 in a court house, both high. Heroin had such a bad hold on me I didn't even have dress shoes to wear. So I ended up stealing a pair from a store on the way to the court house. On March 12, 2009, I was at work dope sick (going through withdrawals), trying to get someone to bring me some dope, but it didn't happen. I got off work, went home, and ended up getting a "buddy" to pick me up to go steal some liquor so I could sell it in order to get myself feeling ok. I had him take me to a store where I went in and grabbed three bottles of champagne. I noticed a guy watching me, but because of my desperation I did not care. I hid the bottles on my body and left the store. I noticed him follow me out to the parking lot. We starting fighting. A couple more security guards came out. Desperation, fear, and hopelessness overtook me. As he and I were fighting, I pulled out a 4 inch knife and stabbed him in the chest. He fell to the ground. I jumped in my buddies van, but he jumped out and acted like he didn't know me. The van stayed surrounded, the police showed up and arrested me. The security guard had a collapsed lung. The blade of the knife missed his heart by 1/16 of an inch, by the grace of God. The security guard made a full recovery after a few days in the hospital.

I was charged with attempted first degree murder, aggravated battery with great bodily harm, aggravated battery with a deadly weapon, and retail theft. I was booked into jail and placed in division 1, the maximum security division. This is where God began to use people to manifest Himself to me. My wife was sitting in jail in a different county in Indiana. She began writing letters telling me about Jesus and the Bible. I responded with, "You're a Bible thumper? I don't want to hear anything about it." She kept on sending scripture and telling me about Jesus, so I thought maybe she was serious about this. I figured we were getting high together, maybe she wasn't going back. I could use the Bible as a way to have something in common with her, since it wasn't going to be drugs anymore. I began to read the Bible. For awhile I thought I came to Christ for the wrong reason. Then God said, "You didn't come to me for the wrong reason. I knew how to get you." Five months after being in jail, it was time for sentencing. The prosecutor was willing to drop the attempt of murder charge and was offering me 8 years. I would have to serve 85% of that. I was praying, family was praying, and God was moving. My public defender said we can take the offer; go to trial, where they had the knife, video, and witnesses; or she could go into a conference with the judge and see what he's offering. It could be better, or it could be worse. I told her go into the conference. When she returned she was in shock. The judge went against what the prosecutor was offering by dropping the attempted murder charge and the aggravated battery with a deadly weapon. He offered 5 years at 50% for aggravated battery with great bodily harm and 3 years for theft. Only God can show favor like that, and I literally just started getting to know Him. He loves you so much that no matter where you are in your walk with him, He is willing to move on your behalf. He will do miracles that only He can do, to let you know it's Him.

I took my time and went to a maximum security penitentiary. I was in my cell 22 hours out of the day. Shortly after being there, God showed favor on me again and allowed me to gain a job that very few people could have. I was there for a year and a half, faithful to church, and bible study, and was used to start two bible studies in a different house. I was finally allowed to be transferred to a medium security penitentiary with more privileges and free movement. I quickly got involved in church, programs, and school. I received my G.E.D. while in prison and gained two more certificates in other classes as well. I was baptized by water submersion in prison and also by the Holy Spirit with evidence of speaking in tongues. God's favor has continued in my life.

Upon coming home in May of 2011, I was able to obtain a job within a month. After being home for three months, while on parole, I was allowed to teach bible study in a jail. I still do this today. Gods allowed me to gain a city job. He has allowed this three time convicted felon and ex-junkie to work as a Corrections Officer. Life is not perfect. There are many trials and storms we go through, but God is always with us. He sees us through the good and the bad. His promises are true. With the foundation of Jesus Christ in your life, there is nothing you can't do. The world will tell you no, but God will tell you yes. He has the final say. Get to know him and have a relationship with Jesus, not religion. I pray that as you read this, you receive what the Holy Spirit is ministering to you and that you become a mighty vessel for God to use. He did it in the life of a heroin addicted thief, with anger and hatred in his heart, who almost killed a man. He can do it in yours if you receive His Son as your Lord and Savior. Love, grace, mercy, peace, and joy are yours if you're willing to give yourself to God.

Want to be free of anger, resentment, and hatred?

Want to be free of drugs and alcohol?

Want out of Satan's grip?

Call out to Jesus right now.

— *Brad*

CHAPTER 27
I Have A
Life Sentence

For many years, I professed Christ in my life...

But Satan was really the master of my heart.

My name is John, heir to salvation and a child of God; a brother in Christ. I am serving an indeterminate sentence in a federal prison in Canada. This means I have a life sentence that does not have a release date, but every few years my detention is reviewed. The Parole Board has the fate of my physical body in its hands, but my soul has already been redeemed by the Blood of Christ, by His grace.

For many years I professed Christ in my life, but Satan was really the master of my heart. I will not glorify Satan by advertising his crimes. I will say this: my crimes were as vile as Satan is vile. His ability to twist the mind and heart is beyond understanding. His presence is a rot in a person's heart. That rot festers and decays your morals, judgment, and reason.

I was raised on the East Coast of Canada, just North of Maine. I came from a large family that was made larger due to the profession of my parents. They operated a foster care group home for the province. At any given time, I had 10-12 other kids in the house. Our household was a staunch Catholic one, where we went to church weekly. As an altar boy, I attended services at times daily.

I spent many of my young years being sexually and physically abused by a couple members of my family. This left me scarred. I grew up without the feeling of true love. I knew a perverse sense of affection but not love.

I left home at a young age and entered the military in Canada, where I was trained and received national certification in cooking. I worked my whole career in the food service industry as a chef and manager.

At this time, I had a dark secret, I had a part of me that did not bring glory to God it was the tool of my destruction that Satan would use to control my life for many years. I do not say that I was not responsible for my actions. I knowingly committed my crimes, and I take full responsibility for my actions. That said though, I know that Satan will use any leverage to keep control of a life, no matter how subtle or seemingly meaningless it looks.

I was arrested in February, 2007 and sentenced on July 4, 2011. During the time while in a pretrial holding, I met regularly with our Chaplain, Jim. I took pride that I was a Christian, but I soon realized that Christ was in my head not in my heart. I started to do some correspondence studies from a couple ministries here in Canada. In studying the word of God I realized that I knew Christ, but he did not know me as I had not made a true commitment to him.

I prided myself in my knowledge. It was in this time God spoke to me through His word in Isaiah 48:7 and Isaiah 47:15. He was telling me that my life could have been different if I had allowed Christ to get out of my head and live in my heart.

Today, Christ lives in my heart. I am at peace, even if He chooses that I remain behind these walls the rest of my life. I now know that Christ lives in me, and I proudly profess Him. The heart is an interesting place. If Christ is not a resident, then Satan is. His presence in your heart is like a spot of rot on an apple. It looks like nothing but give it time and it will overcome that piece of fruit and make it a rotted mess. Satan consumes you by affecting your mind and your judgments, and he decays your morals. He does it in subtle ways so that his control of you is not even something you notice.

There are some who would put degrees or levels of seriousness on sin, but in the eyes of God sin is sin. There is not one sin that is "worse than another." All sin is like filthy rags in the sight of God. People tend to judge the crimes of those around them, but in Gods eyes we are all equal. I mention this because I know the love of God to be blind. All in Christ are commanded to love each other, regardless of their crime. In the Lord's prayer, we ask God to forgive our sins as we forgive the sins of others. We are judged by the same standard that we apply to others.

I hold to the Scripture of 1 Peter 5:7 "Cast all your cares on Him, for He cares for you." Know that He, Jesus, does care for you no matter who you are or what you have done. There is no sin that is so vile that Jesus would be prevented from forgiving. Think about that. Jesus saves and will save ALL who call upon his name. Will you face God's judgment or his Mercy? I have been washed in the blood, and my sins are whiter than snow. Have you been washed in the blood?

Paul called himself the chief of sinners. I felt that I had him beat, but I am a true Child of God, saved by the Blood of Jesus, by His grace and mercy.

— John

It's Time To Pray

If you have already confessed your sins and cried out to God, you are saved. If you have not, it's time that you do. Pray this right now:

Dear God,

I acknowledge You as the Creator of all things. I admit that I am a law breaking sinner, and I deserve the Fires of Hell. I throw myself at Your feet and ask for Your mercy and forgiveness of my sins. I believe that Jesus Christ is Your son. I believe that Jesus died on the cross for my sins and I believe that You raised Him from the dead. Jesus, please come into my heart and fill that place in my heart that belongs only to You. Jesus, I declare You Lord of my whole life today. I will confirm my salvation by telling others what You have done for me. Thank You for saving me!

For more "Real Life Stories," go to the next page. To find out what to do now that you're saved, go to page 139.

CHAPTER 28
Healing
Testimony

I felt pain all over my body....

I was losing so much blood....

My name is Ernest. I was sentenced to a life sentence in 1979. I was sent to Retrieve Unit, and I worked in the kitchen on the slop wagon. I picked up the food waste for the animals to feed. One day my helper did not show up. I lifted these 300 pound cans by myself, up the stairway to the slop wagon. Suddenly, I felt a sharp pain all over my body! I just stood still until the pain went away. I went in the kitchen to speak with my supervisor about giving me a helper to work with. He said that he would send me one. As I turned around to go back to work, the Sgt. called me back and asked why I had red color all over the back of my pants. I told him I didn't know, so I went to the restroom to check on myself. I saw that I was dripping blood from the anus. So I went back to speak to the Sgt. and told him I think I tore something inside of me. He told me to go to the Infirmary and not come back until I was well. I went to the Infirmary, and the nurse said that I was having problems with hemorrhoids. I came to find out that he was wrong. That was not the problem. So I just lay in my bed hoping that the bleeding would just stop. For days, I did not eat or drink anything. I just lay in bed, bleeding. I had lost so much blood, and I felt so weak. The inmates around me called the officers and told them I was bleeding too much. The hospital staff came and carried me away.

I was seen by a doctor. He told the nurses that I was losing too much blood, and I was rushed to the hospital by ambulance. I was admitted and attended to. The next day, I was seen by a doctor and was told that I had a rupture and was going to be examined to look for it. I was taken to a room to be examined by the doctor and they could not locate the rupture. I was sent back to my room and was told that I was going to be back later on that evening. The time came for me to be taken back to the examination room. The doctor worked on me and kept saying, "I can't find it. I don't see it anywhere." It was getting late, and I was told that I was going to be back tomorrow. Morning came, and I was taken back to be examined again. The doctor was getting a little disturbed because he could not locate the rupture. It was getting close to lunch time. I was told that I was going to be back that evening to look for the rupture and get sewed up and sent back to my Unit.

As I was wheeled back to my room, I asked my roommate if it would bother him if I turned on the TV. He said it was okay. As I got the remote control and turned it on, there was an Evangelist Minister speaking. He was saying these words, "There is a prisoner this very moment at a Prison's Hospital that has an internal rupture. The doctors haven't been able to locate it. God has spoken to me to tell you where you are going to find it. It is on the right-hand side of the colon. Right beside it you have full blown cancer. God said to tell the doctor this - that he needs to take that cancer out today or else you are going to die." I could not believe what I was hearing. How did he know about my problem? As I was listening to the man of God, a doctor walked in and with him were eight Texas A & M students. He was telling them about my problems. I looked at the TV. For some reason, the TV was off. I interrupted the doctor's conversation. I said, "Doctor I have something very important to say." He asked, "What is it?" I told him about the man of God that I had heard on TV and what he said as to where he was going to find the rupture. He then asked me, "Okay, where am I going to find it?" I told him what God had said- that it is on the right-hand side of the colon, and that right beside it I had full blown cancer- and that God said he needed to take it out today or else I was going to die, that the cancer was in its last stage.

The doctor looked at me kind of funny, like he didn't really believe what I was telling him. The doctor then had one of the students take me to a room where I was going to have surgery. I waited on the doctor to show up. He walked in and started washing his arms and hands and putting on rubber gloves. He gave me several injections to deaden the parts. Then he started the surgery. He looked for awhile. Then he stopped, got up and walked to the other side of the room. He was talking to some other doctors and nurses who were in the room. Finally, I called to the doctor, and He came back to where I was and said, "I need to speak with you." I asked him, "Did you see the rupture?" He said, "Yes." I asked him, "Did you see the cancer?" He nodded his head, saying yes. I said, "What's the matter, why did you stop?" He said, "The problem is that you're not here for cancer surgery. The cancer is so close to the rupture that, if it should burst, you are a dead man. You have a 50/50 chance that you might make it, and you might not." He said the only way he would be able to work on me is if I would sign some papers stating that he wouldn't be responsible if anything goes wrong. I said, "Give me the papers and a pen. I'll sign them."

I went ahead and signed the papers and gave them back to the doctor. I said, "Doctor, you just do the best you can. I believe God is going to use your hands for His glory." So he started the surgery. He sewed the rupture, and then he asked, "Do you want the cancer gone? Do you want it cut off or burned with a laser?" I told the doctor that he could go ahead and cut it off. He started cutting and got it out of me. He put the cancer in a little tube that they use to get blood out of you. He put the cancer in the tube, showed it to me, and said, "You are a lucky man. Someone up there is looking out for you." I told the doctor, "You are sure right! That someone is God Almighty!! I thank Him so much for giving me another chance in life."

That has been about 32 years ago. About three years ago I was sent to the hospital for examination of any cancer growth. The examination came out negative! There is no sign of cancer in my body- Praise God. I am so thankful that He let me live. God is good, and He is still in the miracle-working business!

PRAISE HIS NAME!

Thank You, Father God, for Your Loving Kindness.

— *Ernesto*

CHAPTER 29
"And Everybody Did What Was Right In His Own Eyes"

That was how I always lived my life; up until 8 years ago when I started to learn about God…….

I grew up in a small country town, and one of my parents always went to church. I went to church also and had a number of Bible books which I read and had read to me. I never approached God with a truthful heart and always went after my own interests.

I was always in trouble as a kid, and I finally was noticed by the police at the age of 11. I was overweight as a kid and never fit in with the other children. I always acted out and did every evil act known to man to get noticed. When I did go to church, I had very little interest and could not wait until it was over. At the age of 15, I stopped going altogether.

All my acts through life have caused others pain and grief, but I was happy as long as I got what I wanted. At the age of 21, I turned into a monster. I drove a tractor-trailer across country and did every hateful thing under the sun to people because I did not think God cared. I lost a lot of weight due to my addiction to speed and alcohol. I tried to form relationships with people, and they all failed. I figured, if the human racce did not care, neither did God.

I lost my license for two DWI's and lost my job. I lost all my toys and my credit and wasted all my money on booze and pills to mask the pain. I felt the only time I liked to be around others was when I was high or drunk. I got a job at a bar and never thought about God being in my life.

ı drank myself to death twice and overdosed on uppers more than once. By the grace of God, He was watching over me, waiting to come back. I never listened. I went about my life and lived it like it was the last day.

I tried to find happiness in a bottle but always turned up empty. I was driving everybody away, even my own family. I got drunk one day and burned down a business. I was now I was wanted for arson. I finally was arrested for that, and still I refused God's offer for help. I was bailed out and went right back to drinking.

In 1998, I killed an innocent man who was my friend. I didn't even know it. I was sentenced to a 15-30 year sentence. God was still watching out for me, but I did not care.

I came to prison with the puffed up frame of mind, that I was a murderer and a tough guy. It took me awhile and a few fights to learn that prison is full of murderers and that taking a life is nothing to brag about.

While I was in prison, I started to take educational classes. I know now, this was part of God's plan. Soon after, about 3 years or so, I was teaching others. I started to change slowly, and God was changing me to fit His will.

One day I came back to my pod, and there was a little Gideons Bible somebody had thrown away. I took it in my cell and slowly started to go through the pages, reading God's word and describing everything I was not.

I went about my time, and soon I received a letter about a Bible Study called Crossroads. I thought, why not, and as I started to do these courses, there was a hunger for more.

I still was afraid that if I turned to God it would show I was weak, but the hunger grew to learn His word. That was many years ago, and a lot of blood and tears wasted on evil thoughts and actions towards people who I was never angry at or had a reason to hate.

I have grown in God's word and have done many school studies. I turned my life over to God. I asked Him to be my Lord and Saviour and to wash me clean.

I have become a minister and have a doctorate in religion through studying His work. I have grown to become a person who does not worry what I am going to get from the world but what I can do for it.

I am planning on devoting the life that God has given me to helping others to avoid jail and prison.

The one thing prison does offer everyone is time to think. A person either thinks about hate or change. I was driving a truck 20 years ago, and I was talking to a driver about my life. He told me if things are not going well without God, maybe it is time to try a different path.

I blew him off by saying, "God does not care. He has enough problems." I can still see that orange cross lit up on the grill of the truck that man was driving.

That has been my lighthouse for the last few years. Things are still bad, but I know that God is there. He offers hope and love. I once read a passage, "The road to salvation is paved with suffering." Suffering is part of life, but now I know God is there to hold my hand and be my best friend.

— *Tobey*

CHAPTER 30
Slave Or Son?
It's Your Choice!

It is a privilege to take a few moments and share with you from my heart. I have been a Chaplain at a jail for 12 Years. I have been going to a Correctional Center for over 15 years. I have done numerous seminars and sessions in the State Prison for several years. As a result of those 25 plus years, I have spent many, many hours in prison. Yet I have never spent one night incarcerated. It is not because I am any better than any one of you reading this message. In fact, in many ways I have done worse things than some of you, but I didn't get caught.

One huge factor is I became a follower of Jesus at the early age of 20. Before that time I was an alcohol addicted, pot smoking, pleasure loving rock and roller. I hit the wall early, and I hit it hard. My life was empty, my heart was heavy, and my 8 month old son lay dying of leukemia. I had no answers, no faith, and no hope. My highest highs couldn't help me. My music couldn't save me. My heart couldn't sustain me.

It is funny how one day, one hour, and one experience can change your life forever. In that moment, I reached upward for the hand of God through Jesus Christ my Lord. He didn't scold me, He didn't ignore me. This poor man cried, and the Lord heard my voice! He gave me new life, new faith, and new love. He showed me that hope sustains and hope fulfills. He showed me that in this world troubles were going to come, but that He would keep me IN everything, THROUGH everything, and never let me down. I turned my life over to Him and He gave me His life and His inheritance. Best of all, HE made me His son, something my orphan heart needed most.

You see in all my years of prison ministry, I believe the key to victory is SONSHIP! Paul wrote this, "And because you are sons, God has sent forth the Spirit of His Son into your hearts, crying out, Abba, Father! Therefore you are no longer a slave but a son, and if a son, then an heir of God through Christ." Gal.4:6-7 According to this there are only two types of people—slaves or sons. The vast majority of us are slaves, living as orphans with no purpose and no identity. We reach for freedom and only experience bondage. Bound to sin, captive to habits, and servants to our own appetites which drive us farther and farther away from God.

Then along comes the consequences of our bad choices. We are arrested, and now alongside our other bondage we lose our last vestige of freedom. Then in our panic we reach out for anything that promises freedom. Make no mistake. Jesus sets people free, but He is not your free ticket to get out. With all my years in prison ministry, by far the most common prayer request is, "Pray for me that I will get out of here." I stopped praying that prayer for men as an initial request years ago. I saw man after man get out only to come back. Some I have ministered to on their fourth bit. This is a result of a wrong definition of freedom. Let's address the real problem, and then we can see the real answer.

First of all the problem is NOT that you are IN prison! The problem is the prison is IN you! Remember Paul's words—we are either slave or son. If this is true and it most certainly is, then something needs to happen deep inside YOU! God can open steel doors and walk people outside the walls of any prison. The fact is most of you reading this will be released some day. But does being outside these prison walls make you free? Certainly not. What is IN you sets the circumstance of life around you. Freedom is a journey within before you ever go out. In fact knowing what freedom is and isn't, is of the utmost importance.

How you define freedom is key to walking in it. Confusion here is deadly. None of us are trying to get more bound. No one sets out as a goal to BE a slave. Yet because we don't understand freedom, we are not free. If the way you understand freedom is from a slave perspective, what you see are steel doors, bars over the windows, guards, towers, and confinement. Therefore, when you get out, you will be free. But the question then is before you were locked up, were you free? Really free? So you see the point is, most of us define freedom in terms of the negative—what we will be when we are no longer locked up. We don't define it in terms of what we could BE or could be doing, but in what we are not.

Why is this important? Because we also see this in terms of habits, sins, and addictions. We define ourselves by what we are NOT doing or have quit doing. If you struggled with drugs or alcohol, we define our freedom by the fact that we quit drinking or drugging. Or if it is an ongoing problem we think I'll be free when I have stopped. Think about Adam in the garden. Was he free? Was it because he didn't drink or do drugs, or cheat on his wife? NO! His freedom was rooted in his IDENTITY! He was a son of God. As long as he walked as a son, he walked free. The moment he lost his identity as a son, he lost his freedom! He didn't define freedom in what he used to do or used to be—but in who he was. Freedom is knowing who I am and in knowing whose I am. Jesus said in Jn. 8:31 "You shall know the truth, and the truth shall make you free."

The knowing of truth is not accumulating the facts but an intimacy through encounter. The truth is not a doctrine to be learned but a PERSON to be known. So our freedom is in encountering and experiencing the Person of Christ and being God's son. Free people are those who step INTO their identity not those who step out of bad habits. Hell will be full of people who quit drinking, stopped doing drugs, or stopped looking at pornography. But heaven will be populated by one kind of person—the free—who stepped into their identity and calling to be sons! Am I saying you don't stop doing those things when you become a Christian? No! But what I am saying is don't just stop something— BECOME something. Don't just get out of prison—get the prison out of you! Don't settle to be a slave—but be a SON! Become a follower of Jesus, and watch where he takes you in Him! 'Therefore if the Son makes you free, you shall be free indeed.' John 8:32

— *Mike Hendon*
mikehendon@citypoint.tv

You Are A New Person

The Bible says:

When someone becomes a Christian, he becomes a brand new person inside. He is not the same any more. A new life has begun!
2 Corinthians 5:17

Say this:

I am a new person. I have a new life, a God centered life.

The Bible says:

All these new things are from God, who brought us back to Himself through what Christ Jesus did. And God has given us the privilege of urging everyone to come into His favor and be reconciled to Him.
2 Corinthians 5:18

God bridged the gap of sin between you and Him by Jesus dying on the cross. He now has given you the honor and privilege of telling people how to find that same favor with God through what Jesus has done for them.

The Bible says:

He died for all so that all who live — having received eternal life from Him --- might live no longer for themselves, to please themselves, but to spend their lives pleasing Christ who died and rose again for them.
2 Corinthians 5:15

Jesus died so you could have eternal life with Him in Heaven. Jesus is calling you to now live for Him, doing only those things with your life that would please Him.

To learn more about what you should now do, go to the next page.

What Do I Do Now?

1. Attend church every time the doors are open.
2. Attend Bible studies.
3. Get a Bible, and read it every day.
4. Pray every day, morning, noon, and night.
5. Tell people what Jesus has done for you.
6. Write out your real life story, your testimony, and give it to people.
7. Make a public profession of your faith by being baptized in water.
8. Shout. Yes, Shout! Friend, you have something to shout about. You've been set free. Death cannot hold you, and Hell can't have you. You belong to God and no matter what happens in this life, as long as you continue to walk with Him, you will be with Him in Heaven...

Church Outreach

Every person that has received Jesus as Savior has a real life story (a testimony).

One of the most effective ways to teach Christians how to share their faith is to get them to write out their testimony (real life story) and share it as part of their every day life style.

Step By Step Ministries, worldwide award winning evangelism teachings are available on DVD and cover the topic of sharing your testimony plus many other effective ways to witness. For more information and resources about witnessing, call, write, or email:

Step By Step Ministries
815 South Babcock Rd.
Porter, IN 46304
219-787-9933

E-mail: Jim@step-by-step.org
website: www.step-by-step.org

Please do not allow this book to become a dust collector.
Take it, and share it with someone.
Allow God to use you to help someone through this book.

Please mail your comments about this book to us at:
Real Life Stories Inmate to Inmate
815 S. Babcock Road • Porter, Indiana 46304

If you would like to read how others in similar situations have experienced the life transforming power of God, please write to me at the address below. We now have over 100 testimonies of those whose lives have been transformed by God's amazing Grace and over 100 Con-Tracts, tracts created by Cons.

Bro. Otto Ball C/o
Crossroads Ministry
P.O. Box 363 • Hyde, PA 16843

If you have a God Glorifying Testimony that you would like to submit to possibly be used in a 3 fold flyer or in our next "Real Life Stories Christian Testimony Book Inmate to Inmate Edition 2," please send it to the above address along with your signed release (see page 143).

- - - - - - - - - - Cut Out & Mail - - - - - - - - - - -

Please pray for me. I have read the "Real Life Stories" Inmate to Inmate Book.

Please check the appropriate box(es):

❑ I prayed and received Jesus as Savior today.

❑ I rededicated my life to Jesus today.

❑ I have questions, and I am searching for answers.

❑ I am born again. I would like to write my testimony and submit it for possible use in a future Inmate to Inmate Book.

Published By
Step by Step Ministries, 219-787-9933
815 South Babcock Road, Porter, Indiana 46304
www.step-by-step.org

------------------------------ Cut Out & Mail ------------------------------

Please Print Name

Place
Stamp
Here

Address

City, State, Zip

Phone

TO: Real Life Stories Inmate to Inmate
815 South Babcock Rd.
Porter , IN 46304

Real Life Stories
And
Step By Step Ministries, Inc.

<u>RELEASE FORM</u>

Date:_____

I hereby authorize *Step By Step Ministries Inc.* to use my written testimony and picture for reproduction in the publishing of Real Life Stories books.

I have read this statement and agree that *Step By Step Ministries Inc.*, their officers, directors, employers, and agents can use the aforementioned and are not to be held responsible for or shall be held harmless for any charges, claims, lawsuits, or liability without limitation.

Name:_____

Address:_____

City:_____ State:_____ Zip Code:_____

Telephone Number:_____

Signature:_____